MOTHER COUNTRY

JEREMY HARDING

Mother Country

A Memoir

faber and faber

First published in 2006
by Faber and Faber Limited
3 Queen Square London WC1N 3AU
This paperback edition published in 2007

Typeset by Faber and Faber Limited
Printed in England by Mackays of Chatham plc, Chatham, Kent

A CIP record for this book is available from the British Library

ISBN 978–0–571–21294–1
ISBN 0–571–21294–8

2 4 6 8 10 9 7 5 3 1

Contents

Preface vii

Preface

I was about five when I learned I'd been adopted. Ever since, I've had one or another version of the event in my mind, or at the back of it. There were times when it was intriguing, others when it looked like an advantage in life, others still when it seemed to complicate my world unduly. I'd thought often about looking into the family I hadn't known. Years went by and, in the end, my not getting round to it convinced me that I never meant to do so.

Adoption is more than a story about the fate of obscure mothers and absentee fathers, or resettled children and the lives they go on to lead. And the bigger the story, to my way of thinking, the better. I was discouraged by the idea of turning up a few meagre pieces of the past – other people's past – that were too special to throw away, but couldn't be matched with any larger picture of the way a society thinks about parents and children, and how this changes over time. My inertia was compounded by beliefs I held about blood and kinship: it wasn't obvious to me that the blood tie mattered. I liked to think that if families worked, it was because they'd gone about inventing themselves in the right way, which was largely a question of luck. Mostly I still feel that.

Even so, something changed over the years. I became easier with the idea of retrieving a handful of fragments and looking at them in their own right. Indeed, I'd become eager to fill what I thought was a blank in the record by making some attempt to find out who my natural mother had been and whether I really did have sisters, as one of the stories about her went. Then there were my own children: it seemed right to try to establish something on their account. It was an interesting story, just possibly, and if it could be told to them, it would show that people were joined up, and separated, in all sorts of ways. Kinship by blood must therefore have become an intelligible thing to me.

On my own account, I expected to write something about the mother I'd not known, to piece together her portrait, and to set it somewhere – in a notebook or a folder – along with what I'd been told about her, and thought about her, when I was a boy. I imagined something like an obituary. It was important that my adoptive father was no longer alive and my adoptive mother was too infirm to know what I was doing.

I started the investigation off in 1998 with a few legal formalities. I continued, intermittently, while I was living in London. (All the early lines of enquiry seemed to link my natural mother to the capital, at least in the years directly after I was born.) Shortly afterwards, I moved to France, and didn't get back to England much until the winter of 2002, when I went to stay with friends in London, and set about trying to discover something hard and fast about my natural family.

What follows is largely the story of those two periods. The first, desultory phase, beginning in 1998; and the second, a hectic tumble through the city four years later, when some unlikely bits and pieces began to emerge, by no means all of them about my natural relatives. I say a lot about my adoptive family. Partly that's because I owed many of my early fancies about my natural mother to the things that my adoptive mother said about her. Partly because those things were among the evidence I had to go on. Then, too, in the course of looking for information about my natural family, I stumbled on new information about the one I'd grown up with.

A search of this kind is supposed to be methodical. But the method is bound to involve a certain madness. I've tried to give a sense of the spectral realms you enter when you're looking for people you don't know, about whom there's little in the way of hard fact. Wild conjecture is always ready to fill in the gaps or lead the way to comic misunderstandings. Adoption has any number of those. Meanwhile the people you lived with – and thought you knew – come out of the past asking to be revisited, or even addressed. What are we to say to the dead? That we might have loved them better?

This is a book about mothers and fathers, real and imagined – and about two mothers in particular. Thinking about mothers seems to me to be like straying into 'Indian country': tricky terrain for small boys and aspiring men trying to work out the geography. The pitfalls are not really to do with mothers themselves and there's no obvious struggle going on, as there was in the case of native American lands: no wagon trains and cavalry detachments trespassing avidly on ancestral ground. Even so, the contours of 'Mother Country' are sometimes daunting, and knowing where you are or quite who's out there can be hard, since to some extent the child creates the mother in its mind – a charmed, unreliable place, where real people and events undergo strange transfigurations. One of my mothers was so eccentric as to seem like a figment of several different imaginations, including hers and mine. The other was, for most of my life, a mother of the mind. I'm not sure we can ever say much that's useful about the people we carry in our heads until we've managed to see them as people in the world, as I've tried to do here.

As for my own mother country, Britain, it's ground on which I can venture with more confidence, even though I've lived abroad for a while – or because I have. Class and the theatrical attitudes it asks us to strike play a big part in this story – bigger than I could ever have forseen – which may simply mean that it's a very English story. Class consciousness was a powerful force in the 1950s and '60s, when I was growing up, and I'm not convinced that the extraordinary changes of the last thirty or forty years have turned the British class system into a heritage site. So I've had something to say, obliquely, about the embarrassment and exoticism (and irony) of class denominations in the mother country to which I'm so attached. I suppose they're part of the broad picture I used to think might never emerge from an excavation of this type. Maybe what I've found isn't just an assortment of odds and ends after all.

A few names in this account have been changed with a view to preserving the privacy of people whose lives I burst in on. In several cases, minor details of fact have been altered. One result of giving people pseudonyms is that passages in this book no longer square with the public record. There won't be a Drew, for instance, at the house number given on Wembley Park Drive in the late 1950s. These discrepancies are left to stand. As for the places I grew up in and the people who looked after me, I've made one or two discreet changes and altered the spelling of a name.

The use of 'birth', as in 'birth-mother', has been avoided. 'Natural' is no longer favoured in discussions about adoption, but it has one great advantage: it's hard to use without the antithetical sense of 'culture' coming to mind. Adoption – to wrest the monopoly of wonders from nature – is one of the marvels of culture. Another, I stubbornly persist in thinking, is the fact that a mother may feel something like love for her biological children throughout her life, whether they're insistently present, or torn away from her by circumstance at an early stage. We tend to think a mother's love is 'only natural', but there may be more to it than that.

MOTHER COUNTRY

Names

The name of my natural mother was Margaret Walsh. It's on the birth certificate I have on the desk and which I'm looking over for the first time in my life, a spring morning in London, 1998. It appears twice, first under column five, 'Name, surname and maiden surname of mother', and then under column seven, as the person registering the birth. The address of Margaret Walsh the 'informant' is off Ladbroke Grove in west London, a neighbourhood I know quite well, and this is probably where she was living around the time of my birth. The address given under Margaret Walsh the mother doesn't appear to be hers: it's a premises, most likely a very small shop, in a very small close about two miles away, in the London Borough of Hammersmith, where she was working as a 'counter assistant' in the summer of 1952.

It was Ann Pike, an adoption counsellor, who told me to apply for the birth certificate. She did so at our first meeting, a few weeks before, in her office at the Family Records Centre in Clerkenwell. Having a social worker seemed as unlikely to me as winning a medal for services rendered to the Empire, but I couldn't have got the original certificate of my own birth without her. And it wouldn't have been possible before Section 26 of the Children Act 1975, which acknowledged, in effect, that the state could not close every door to adopted people with an interest in their past. The right to a copy of an original birth certificate, reiterated in the Adoption Act 1976, marked a very significant change in favour of the inquisitive adoptee, even if the disclosure of more detailed information was left to the discretion of the courts and adoption agencies.

It nonetheless compromised the understanding on which many mothers had parted with infants: they had been told that the children they gave up for adoption were unlikely ever to trace them, or even to ascertain their surnames. For this reason anyone adopted before 1975 who wants to know more about the circumstances of the adoption, or indeed to trace a parent, is legally obliged, in the words of a document prepared by the Office for National Statistics, to 'see an experienced social worker called a counsellor' before obtaining the crucial piece of evidence on which to proceed – the original birth certificate.

The certificate fixes my birth on 7 July 1952 – a matter of doubt when I was a boy. Until the age of seven, when I went away to school, I seemed to have been born on 5 July. Then it changed, and my eighth birthday, the first of many away from the adoptive family, fell on 7 July. It's good to see the seventh reaffirmed – I wouldn't care to go back to the fifth after all these years. But there are surprises.

It states on the certificate that the child was born in Hammersmith Hospital. My adoptive mother used to say it was St Mary's Paddington. Then there is the given name Jeremy. For years I'd assumed my name was a badge of my adoptive parents' pretensions, a matter of social fashion: there are a lot of Jeremys, Julians, Adrians and Timothys from that era. Why a working woman - in Ann Pike's opinion an Irishwoman, as my adoptive mother had always said - would want to give a name like Jeremy to the child she was about to hand over is a puzzle.

Finally, not so much a surprise as a shock, there is the single short dash, the kind you use to mark a hyphen – one clack of a key through the typewriter ribbon – under 'Name and surname of father'.

At the bottom of the document is a statutory warning in bold red capitals:

THIS CERTIFICATE IS NOT EVIDENCE OF THE IDENTITY OF THE PERSON PRESENTING IT.

There was Maureen, of Maureen and Colin – my adoptive parents the Hardings – and there was the natural mother, who's referred to by adoption experts as the 'birth mother': the first mother, that's to say, who then becomes the eternal mother-in-hiding. But you wouldn't – I wouldn't – really want to say 'my mother' about either, even though I do. Then there's adoption, another difficult word. 'My adoption'? It sounds like an affliction, or a misfortune, though it was far from being either.

I seem to see Maureen, Mother Two, walking up a set of steps on to a raised wooden deck in front of a shingled house with double doors leading into a boxy living room. The blonde hair is well arranged, the eyebrows have been tended, making them dark and thin. She's humming, 'I'd risk everything for one kiss, everything . . .' But the memory isn't accurate. That song was written much later, after we'd moved out of the house I'm thinking of. Mother Two seems resolute, indifferent to almost everything but the double doorway and the tune I can't put my finger on.

And Margaret Walsh? Of her there is no image grounded in the memory of a real place. There is only the fact of a brief physical connection severed long ago. Mother One is elusive, which is perhaps what makes her interesting. There may also be brothers and sisters – and of course there was a father – with whom I have no material connection at all beyond blood. I'm still not sure why blood should matter or why we continue to repeat the platitude about blood and water. When I was younger, I didn't like to hear it said that one was thicker than the other. I reasoned against it and finally denied it on principle.

For long periods of my childhood, I grew up with the fact of water. I was raised by a river. 'Thick' is a good word for the way water seemed to me when I was young and still seems now: sustaining, brown, benign – or white, decisive, invigorating, rushing over a weir, churning from the back of a boat. Having been adopted, I was spared the binding notion of blood, with all its passion and fatalism. I simply took the platitude and stood it on its head. I am no longer sure what to think, except that this interest in origins is a perversity on my part, like going back over a dispute that was settled years ago.

Doubly perverse because of my debt to water. I owe nothing to blood, but I owe a great deal to the eccentric couple who adopted me in London and then carted me off to a world of slippery

landing stages, locks and leaking boats, flooded fields and impass-
able roads. I've no idea what I owe to my lost progenitors – the
absent father and the enigmatic Mother One, who conceived and
bore me, and for one reason or another decided to leave it at that.
And wouldn't the wise course be to do the same – to leave it at
that? There's always an unsettling sense that the urge to know
more about Margaret Walsh is disloyal, not just to Colin and
Maureen, but to the life I lived with them and the course that life
went on to take.

At our second meeting, Ann Pike was neither encouraging nor
discouraging. She felt that looking for evidence of Margaret Walsh
would be hard but not impossible. She urged me to think about
my own family, to turn over the past for any sort of clue. She
wanted, for her part, to know a little about Colin and Maureen
Harding. I answered with a short summary I have at the ready. I
referred to them, as I always have, as my mother and father. As I
was speaking, I seemed to see their little boy clearly. Not an
importunate figure, not someone whose own understanding was
being traduced by what I had to say, but an insistent creature, who
might want to add a remark, or urge me to think more carefully as
I spoke.

Had I gone on to explain in detail how things were between
Colin and Maureen and that small boy, I'd have said that the
grown-ups were uncomfortable with the subject of how he came
to be with them. And that as time wore on, they may have misre-
membered the details of the story. I forget whether I told Ann that
I was a secret. As far as Colin's parents knew, Maureen had given
birth to the bright new member of the family in a London clinic.
This make-believe must have been hard to keep up, especially
since Colin and Maureen already had the use of a flat below
Colin's parents for several months of her slim-line pregnancy,
which ought by rights to have begun in the winter of 1951.

For Maureen especially, the adoption was a source of other,
steeper fantasies, which she divulged in fits and starts. Much of
what she said was unreliable, I realise now. She liked to tell vivid

and abrupt tales about her own past. But the elementary versions of the adoption story – the ones she began telling her little boy when he was about five – weren't in the least deceitful. And perhaps her stories got more impressive as they acquired more detail, in subsequent retellings. Or maybe they got blowsier, like Maureen herself, and altogether less reliable.

To the happy child, at ease by the water, there was something marvellous about the early versions of the story: the glimmerings of a fable, as I'd understand later, the tale of a life redeemed from hardship and poverty – a class fable, to be sure. But these early versions, and there are two I recall, were simple. They must have been well told, and carefully prepared for the ears of a small boy. In any case, they had a powerful effect on me: by the time I was six or seven, my sense of the world we lived in had undergone a dramatic enlargement, stretching beyond the river, and the apartment in London, to a place full of obscure difficulty where a young woman, poor but kind, had given up a baby.

I don't suppose my sense of our life by the water was something Colin and Maureen shared. Theirs was an adult world and by definition more complicated. It was also more contradictory. Colin was a sociable creature, as Maureen was in the early days. They loved parties and drink and golf and nightclubs. There was a deal of upbeat coming and going with friends and acquaintances, and a slightly edgier mixing with the people Colin knew from the narrow world of contract bridge. But over the years he managed to fall out with many of his friends and at the heart of his festive disposition a marked indifference to other people seemed to lurk – not that he wished his friends ill, but he often wished them elsewhere.

He loved his rundown establishments by the river more than he loved London. He was happy to be cut off from the world, to live in a cloister of tattered privileges and ever-improving creature comforts, sealed off by embankments, impenetrable towpaths and sodden gardens. The water that enveloped our habitat was a guarantee of privacy; and so, despite Colin and Maureen's friends, and the many winter weekdays spent in the flat below his parents in

Notting Hill, ours was the moated life. As I got older, I began to think of the Hardings as moat-people. People, that's to say, who felt comfortable – disdainful, above all – so long as they were well dug in.

Yet the element that coddled and secluded us could also undo us, creeping up, slipping closer, so that you'd open the curtains on a Saturday morning, the day after you'd got down from London, to find yourself cut off. This process of watery insinuation went on, year after year, until I was about twelve. In time, I grew to believe that our riverside life had worked a bad magic on Colin and Maureen and a benign magic on me. I can still see the water pressing up over the banks of the river, still sense Colin's odd mixture of satisfaction and impatience, Maureen's misery and discomfort, and feel my own barely stifled pleasure as the levels kept rising. Whether or not Colin and Maureen were once fun loving, gregarious people, I must have decided a very long time ago, heartlessly, that I was a free spirit and they were marooned. That my life was real and theirs was not. Affable, good with the cocktails, but the loneliest couple you'd ever come across is how I thought of them.

Letters are written. Institutions and people are approached. That is the routine work of an adoption inquiry. Words are repeated – 'birth mother', for instance – and assurances are given. 'I am aware of the issues,' I write at the end of more than one letter, meaning that I'm unlikely to cause embarrassment or mayhem in the near future. It is a non-language, this talk about 'issues'. It honours our superstitious sense of the self as an unstable infant hiding in the folds of the adult person: a self that does not grow old like the organs, and needs to be chivvied towards death and other less draconian kinds of maturity.

Ann Pike did not speak in this way. She talked generously and practically about the obstacles I was likely to encounter, warning of false starts and blind alleys. She reminded me that I could abandon the investigation at any time if it seemed to be overwhelming, or fruitless, or depressing. She pointed out more than once that there was a fair chance Margaret would be dead by now. I said, 'I understand that.' (Another social worker might have got us to agree that this was an 'issue'.) I wanted to say that I knew Margaret was dead.

For a fact?

No, but I knew in the way you know, before you've begun going through your pockets, that you've left your keys somewhere. I'm not sure I'd have had the nerve to start looking for her otherwise. I wanted to tell Ann I planned to write something: a tribute, a few words on paper about a woman I'd never known.

II

Places

Summer 1998 and I'm heading for one of the addresses on my birth certificate. A loose-fitting, sunny August morning. Manageable traffic.

I have the certificate on the passenger seat of the car, next to a notepad. I imagine the original document being filled out by a typist in some cheerful office where the rudimentary facts about human beings go on the record: they are born, they are named, they marry, reproduce and die. The details are certified so that each of us has a recognisable status in law and the massive documentation which enables a society to know something about itself remains up to date. Under the heading 'Name, if any', the typist enters 'Jeremy', hits the space-bar four or five times and enters 'Boy' under the heading 'Sex'. The carriage moves on a few more spaces, to column four, 'Name and surname of father'. One finger of the left hand depresses the shift key and another on the right snaps out a dash.

Under column five ('Name, surname and maiden surname of mother'), my typist moves on to an exposition of character, naming a principal, assigning her a job and a place of work: 'Margaret Walsh, Counter Assistant, Chain Stores, of 43, Mackenzie Close, Hammersmith'. On from there to column six: 'Occupation of father'.

Again, a single dash.

Then column seven: development of the character in column five, or else the introduction of a second character – all this under 'Signature, description and residence of informant'.

In this case it was the mother who doubled as the informant, and so the typist confides a second vital detail about the main protagonist: 'MARGARET WALSH, Mother, 22, Chesterton Road, W10'. There is not, of course, a signature. I am not even sure whether the puzzling rubric 'signature' means 'signed name'.

Finally the word 'Adopted' appears over the name of the registrar, which is where the story ends.

This is what there is to go on.

Ann Pike took the question of paternity to be a bigger question to do with Margaret and the kind of girl she was. She spoke of the 1950s as a time of placements for single mothers, unmarried women with unwanted pregnancies: lodgings for women who'd wandered from the path; hostels for stray persons who were hosts themselves to not-yet-persons. For people who want to find out about their adoption, the mother is the information gateway, even if she's only a name on a piece of paper. And a mother in Margaret Walsh's circumstances, or the circumstances Ann surmised, would have been under pressure to disclose the name of the father, even if she'd wanted nothing more to do with him. It was seen as the proper procedure, a matter of record.

How much pressure?

Ann was uncertain. But it would have come from the borough or county council that handled the adoption, and from the carers – nuns, or some other order of charitable persons – who lodged and fed a bevy of post-war single mothers. Pressure, then, was the right word, and the absence of the father's name on the certificate suggested a dogged wish on Margaret's part to withhold it. I saw no reason why she should have had to divulge the name of any third party, even if it might have helped me establish something about her now.

And what if her reticence wasn't deliberate? What if she hadn't known the name of the man in question? The answers to these questions might lie anywhere, but they had their origin in London. It was in London, as far as I knew, that Margaret conceived her little boy. And, as he got older – six or seven maybe – as he heard more fragments of his unlikely story from Maureen, it was London that seemed to contain Margaret, to reckon her in its vast, chaotic accounting, hidden but probably safe.

Number 22 Chesterton Road stands on the corner of St Lawrence Terrace, an ample house with a porch and columns, a mile or more north of Colin's parents' house, where we'd had the flat until I was about six.

At the time I was born, the serial killer John Reginald Christie was a resident of Rillington Place, on the other side of Ladbroke Grove from Chesterton Road. Years after Christie was hanged, having first confessed to the murder of seven women, he must have posed a lingering threat, or sufficed as a terrible example: I can recall his name in the conversations Colin and Maureen had when we were still in the flat. Of course, I knew nothing of Christie's doings, or the possibility that he'd pinned one of his crimes on a neighbour. But I do recall the attractive sound of 'Christie', and the puzzling idea of a hanging, which became linked in my mind with *The Tale of Mr Tod* by Beatrix Potter. In this frightening story, which Colin used to read to me and which I always begged to hear again, Mr Tod the fox returns home to find Tommy Brock the badger sleeping in his bed. He suspends a metal pail from one end of a clothes line above the badger and ties the other to a tree outside. He fills the pail with water while Tommy Brock snores on, or seems to, and when all is ready, he returns to the tree and gnaws through the rope with his teeth. The pail of water crashes on to the intruder below. This is part of what I imagined happening to Christie.

But Tommy Brock had seen it coming. He had bundled up a dressing gown and put it in the bed, to make it look as though he were still there, and then he'd sneaked into the kitchen. I learned when I was older that Christie had eluded the hangman first time around: the pail had come hurtling down on Timothy Evans, another tenant at 10 Rillington Place. When Christie's enormities had all been unearthed, the public's sense that an innocent man had already been punished in his stead darkened the story further.

In Christie's day, 22 Chesterton Road might well have been a charitable home for single women in the closing stages of pregnancy, tiding them over and eventually seeing them on their way. This was Ann Pike's first hunch about the address on the certificate, although neither of us had found anything in the record to suggest she was right.

I walked down towards Ladbroke Grove, returned and stood outside the house. It had been converted to create a separate lower ground floor flat. A brown yucca plant was set on the first-floor balcony and big tubs of rosemary on the ground-floor window ledge. In the area window of the basement flat were some smaller pot plants and a couple of children's toys. I imagined the view through the same window years before. More austere; dusty perhaps. And if I went with Ann's instincts, a nun was coming down the stairs to chide the caretaker.

In fact, moments later, it was a young woman in a red sweater with a baby on her arm who walked to the sink behind the sash and ran the tap.

I sat in the kitchen at home with a notepad open on the sideboard. It was all but empty.

Following Ann's suggestions in a general sort of way, I tried to remember when my father – not Colin, but Margaret Walsh's lover – had entered the picture. It was via Maureen, no doubt about that, at a time in our lives when the first telling of the adoption story – which I'll come to – had already happened and the lesser tellings, or embellishments, were now in order. I'd guess I was thirteen or fourteen. I'm not sure how the conversation went.

'Your father', Maureen seems to be saying, 'was a waiter, I think, or a what's-its-name, you know, a steward, on a . . . what I call a Scandinavian ship.'

'What I call' was one of Maureen's most memorable expressions. It gave her a good deal of licence. She might use it while naming a perfectly familiar object, in which case it seemed to endow her with distinction and consign the object in question to everlasting banality ('It's what I call a lawnmower'). Or she might use it when she felt that what she had to say was true but difficult ('He's what I call a layabout'). Or she might flourish it like a white flag: I have a rough idea what I mean and you'd do well to follow my drift, because if you want to set me straight, I may have trouble following yours.

Scandinavia was a case of the white flag that didn't quite mean surrender.

'He might have been Norwegian – or, you know, a Belgian. Or what's the other one up there?'

In any case Scandinavia appealed to me.

'He must have been dashing, darling,' says Maureen, trying to cast him in an agreeable light. 'I mean, if he's anything like you'll be – you wait till that thing's come off your teeth.'

Which helps with the dates, now I think of it. They had my teeth fixed quite late; and I used to take the brace out to do boxing; and I boxed for the last time when I was fourteen. I was the child of a hardy Scandinavian sailor, which suited me fine.

A day or so after I'd been to Chesterton Road, I decided to explore Mackenzie Close, the other address on the certificate. Under a gauze of cloud filtering the morning sunlight, I parked the car on one of the bigger roads that crossed the White City Estate, just south of the A40.

The very thought of this estate would have sent a ripple of anxiety through the water in our moat when I was a boy. A massive public housing project of the sort Colin detested, it was conceived in the 1930s as part of an ambitious scheme to replace the substandard housing in which so many working-class London families lived. And it has rolled on for more than half a century as a monument to the idea that well-built working-class housing is something a society might be proud of. You can feel the period grandeur – the admirable weight of that ambition – as you walk the estate, though it's by no means the desirable place that it was at the end of the Second World War.

Mackenzie Close, where Chain Stores, Margaret's shop, was once situated, had the air of a large courtyard rather than a close, and there was no sign of any store. It must have disappeared years ago to make way for a residential extension. The housing here was in dark brick. Above the ground floor a walkway gave access to a dozen flats. It began raining. I retreated to the shelter of an ash tree and waited, as if for someone I knew. A black teenager in a tracksuit jogged past, his head covered by a grey flannel hood, his face divided by a glistening fissure of sweat and rain. He smiled and ducked into the entranceway of the flats, the clap of his trainers echoing in the concrete stairwell. In the rain, the roar of the traffic on the Westway, about fifty yards off, had been tamped down into an incessant hiss.

From the first laws on adoption in England and Wales in 1926 until the Children Act of 1975, the notion was to put up a nearly impregnable barrier – nowadays we'd say a 'firewall' – between the original family and the adoptive family. Quite apart from helping the natural mother to make the best decision for her child (she wouldn't have to explain herself later, and why should she?), this was thought to have obvious advantages for the new mother and father, clearing away any ambiguities about their status as parents. A child's best interests seemed to lie in the straightforward assertion that it belonged legally, morally and emotionally with its adoptive family and no other. As a result, children who were told of their adoption would have found it hard to discover who they might 'really be', or who their natural parents 'really were'. But after the changes in the law, they could ask these questions with a view to proper answers. The original birth certificate that an adopted person was now entitled to see could lead eventually to living people, or a history of dead ones.

Colin and Maureen were beneficiaries of the 'closed' adoption policies of the day. And so was Margaret Walsh's little boy. That those policies happened to suit their requirements was a stroke of luck. Moat-people, as I'd come to see them, might as well be thought of as 'firewall-people'. Colin and Maureen would have been dismayed to think their adopted child might want to find Mother One, and horrified to think he might even find her: that would not have been playing by the rules. In this much, they went along with the adoption consensus.

Going along was seldom Colin's way. In most respects, he thought himself above the world of law and policy. Rules in general, from speed limits to the rudimentary forms of courtesy – these were for little people. And they were all in their ways intrusions on a bigger man's right to privacy, as indeed was the very idea of public planning – of the public at all. By the mid-1960s, the word 'sociology' could not be spoken in our house without a whine of disapproval, as though we were under assault. In general, Colin's politics were outlandish. Though he might poke fun at any one of his heroes, he admired strong right-wing government, General Franco's and the Greek junta in particular. He was fiercely opposed to any social arrangement that might keep disadvantaged people alive too long and put a burden on more fortunate families like ourselves.

In a perfect world, I think he would have taken the thrust of 'closed adoption' to exuberant extremes by obtaining a child of the desired gender for a fee negotiated in private, and then paid a premium to have the natural mother shot.

More fortunate families. I find it difficult to place Colin according to the rigours and foibles of the British class system. How he and Maureen thought of themselves – how we all thought of ourselves for many years – is another matter: in our own eyes, we were undoubtedly rather grand. The money on Colin's mother's side came from dentistry: a relative with some distinguished patients, including – it was said – the Queen. On Colin's father's side there was no shortage of wealth either. I am not sure where the money came from, though I've an idea how it was spent. For it was also said that my grandparents were a prodigal pair in their youth and lost an enormous sum in Monte Carlo shortly after they were married in 1913. Ten years later, they lost the better part of another fortune at the same tables, so the story went. But like much that was said in the family, it was a partial truth: for the remainder of their lives, Colin's parents were able to live in comfort and, occasionally, splendour. It was mostly in that splendour that I came to know them, Colin's mother especially, who saw very little point in Colin and rather less in Maureen, though she took a shine to me.

Colin's mother was open and apparently carefree, but she liked a dispute and loved a lawyer: often, as I got older, I'd come upon her writing long letters to her solicitor in the same difficult hand I'd enjoyed deciphering when I was a boy. The closing stages of her letters were especially tricky. The text moved down the last page in the ordinary way and then, on reaching the bottom, turned through ninety degrees to scale the right-hand margin to a width of three lines, turning again at the top, the characters now decidedly smaller and the sheet itself upside down. Finally a swift descent was effected in the left-hand margin, finishing with a bump in the bottom corner, which always took the same affectionate form. It was only as she was coming to the end of a thing that Colin's mother ever seemed to get the measure of it – which must have accounted for her vivacity in the last years of her life, as well as her love of puddings. I've no idea what she wrote to her lawyers about – wills possibly, contentious rights of way near her own property or minor disagreements with the local authority.

Colin's mother was known as Mim. This is what everyone called her, though from an early age I thought of her in a cool, proprietorial way as my grandmother – something of mine more than anything of Colin's. She was fond of birds. She put out regular supplies of lamb fat and bacon rind hung on a kind of clothes line; she tamed moorhens and brought ducks into the house – through the main room, along into the kitchen and sometimes upstairs – which was thought to be shocking. Dressed in a shabby, last-minute way, seldom without a hairnet to complete the effect, she was nevertheless oddly elegant, and gave the impression that at some point in the early morning, making haste and running riot had been the only options: there were the birds to attend to, there was the garden and at length the solicitor. She looked a little like the end of one of her letters. Sleeves were prolonged by stray pieces of fabric which would then be wound around a forearm and tucked in at the first opportunity, such as a hole at the elbow. It was the same with hems, from which large flanks would fall obstinately free until they were retrieved and pinned freestyle on to her skirts. Higher up, a pretty clasp held her numerous cardigans and wraps suspended on the brink of disarray.

Her family – the Montague-Smiths – had undoubtedly looked smarter. They'd worked their way up in the world, and striven to maintain a position which she showed no sign of relinquishing, even though she dressed a little strangely, and kept a hot water bottle under her coat, and was once found, during a visit by the family doctor, with three ducks in her bed. Colin's father, on the other hand, was apt to let things slide. Or to hope they'd remain where they were with a minimum of effort. He worked for the Coal Board, having come in, I guess, through a private coal company when the industry was taken into public ownership. He was a keen gambler and golfer, and he liked to drink.

Colin was much the same. He had enjoyed his undergraduate days, played bridge for his university and scraped a law degree. The Second World War put paid to his ambitions at the bar and after demobilisation he proceeded to do very little until, finally, he joined the Stock Exchange. Despite his lack of height, he was a good-looking man, and despite being strapped for cash in the early days, he kept up payments to his tailor. Often enough, in a British black-and-white film made in the 1940s or early 1950s, there'll be a scene in a drawing room that brings the main protagonists and the bit parts together. A well-educated, slightly dubious character of minor significance to the plot will stand near the mantelpiece and deliver a line that livens up the dialogue while lowering the tone. He'll have a drink in one hand and a cigarette in the other. There is an easy charm about this character and somewhere a willingness to play fair, if only he were in a position to dictate the rules.

That is Colin. And that's the kind of people we probably were.

III

Fables

By the time I next met Ann Pike, it was obvious that there was little to go on. Our efforts in the interval had turned up nothing encouraging. She was sure now that no agency had been involved in the adoption. Most likely it had been done privately. Private adoptions were hard to unravel at a distance of fifty years. The next step, she suggested, was to apply to the courts for permission to see the file on the adoption.

> 17th July 1998
>
> I am writing to ask whether the Court would consider making further information available about the details of my adoption in 1952/3. I put this request on the advice of Ann Pike, my Adoption Counsellor at the Family Records Office. Following the return by the Court of the CA6 form, which referred us to the London County Council records, nothing has come up at the Metropolitan Archives. There are no records, either, with the borough social services.
>
> I've already identified the name of my birth mother, Margaret Walsh, and, having put the process under way, I'm reluctant to let it drop. I've received the statutory counselling and I'm aware of the issues.
>
> Yours etc

The reinforced window of the waiting room at the West London County Court carried a printed message from the Clerk to petitioners about how to avoid what were clearly unavoidable delays. By the Clerk's signature someone had scrawled 'barstad' in permanent felt-tip. Ann Pike looked disconsolately at the coffee I'd fetched from the machine. She'd hoped for a preliminary conversation with the judge who'd agreed to the hearing – case number J748 – but as it turned out, he wasn't there. The district judge presiding did not have 'family jurisdiction' and could not rule on my request. It was an autumn day in London. The mist of the early morning had given way to drizzle. People came and went in the hall behind us. Umbrellas were shaken out or readied for the fray. I wanted most of all to walk across to the Clerk's notice and correct the spelling of 'bastard'.

Over the next few days I thought a lot about my childhood. I felt I should probe for a core of unhappiness beneath what were mostly happy memories, but I didn't find one.

It's true that when Colin and Maureen sent me to boarding school, at the age of seven, a kind of screen came down between us. Indeed, we lost each other at that point and none of us really found a way back. This is not always the effect of boarding at an early age, but it was in my case. By the time I was ten, the parents I'd doted on were a blur in the middle distance. So were Jill and Peter, the two children of Maureen's previous marriage. I'd seen little of them – they too were boarders and spent much of their holidays with their father in Surrey – yet I'd grown very attached to them early on. Peter, a beautiful, curly-haired creature, was thirteen years older than me; Jill, a blonde replica of Maureen, perhaps ten.

Until that major separation, I can remember very few disruptions in the almost eerie fluency of my contentment, living in the care of an easygoing, shiftless couple who kept a base in London and moved from one to another of their ragged riverside properties, on land bounded by the Thames and a narrow tributary called the Loddon, which Colin's mother and father had acquired thirty or forty years earlier.

'Properties' is the wrong word – too illustrious for the three or four adjacent plots with buildings in wood and cement that went through a slow series of improvements – electricity for instance – until they were nearly comfortable.

It was a few yards from one of the less tumbledown billets, known as Rosemary Cottage, that I had my first real encounter with a river. It was an ordeal by water – a moment of terrible alertness rather than misery or fear – from which I emerged unharmed but mysteriously indebted.

Colin's mother had named the cottage after his sister, though Rosemary scarcely ever lived in it. In those days, apparently, we had a right to it: Colin had a right to help himself to anything belonging to Rosemary. The cottage was set back a few yards from the Loddon, which joined the Thames about a quarter of a mile below the garden. There was a willow growing out into the water, where it led a horizontal existence in partial immersion, at a slight curve in the bank. In summer, when the current was leisurely, I would walk up and down along this cambered causeway which stopped abruptly about fifteen feet from the bank. From time to time, I would twirl on the branches that grew vertically from the prone trunk. In winter, before the floods engulfed it completely, I was more cautious. The water was higher and the current swift, tearing at the submerged head of the tree and straining in frantic little eddies on its downstream side.

For a couple of winters we remained mostly at the cottage and I was put in a friendly little school a few miles away. I'd have been four or five. In the late afternoons, after I was fetched home, I used to go down to the tree, in spite of stern warnings from Maureen. It was slippery, but I could straddle my way along it and settle into position with my boots a few inches from the roil. With a stick I'd prod the formations of scum by the edge of the trunk, fascinated by that forbidding surface – the Loddon was always a dun colour, sullen even in its haste – until dusk turned to darkness, the lights went on in the cottage behind me and Maureen, or the nanny from Germany, summoned me indoors.

'How many times have I told you not to go out along the willow?'

On a grey, midwinter day I finally lost my footing. I was aghast at the cold, out of my depth and carried, helplessly, into a small enclave behind the tree. Now and then I seized at the grass on the side of the bank, but the tug of the current and the weight of my waterlogged clothes dragged out my handholds by the roots. I struggled and shouted, and fought for fresh ones. I was dimly

21

aware that someone had set out from a landing stage on the opposite bank – a matter of twenty or thirty yards, but the current bore against the boat. He had to wrestle it back upstream and coax it round the flank of the tree, and I remember a voice urging me to hang on. I thrashed and fought in the hectic brown water. I'd torn most of the grass from the side of the bank and was now sinking my fingers into wet, root-veined earth. The final two or three holds were mud.

I grasped the flat bow of the punt with one hand and reached up with the other, to be hauled over the side, drenching the boards. I was sobbing and shuddering. I had lost a boot, and remember thinking that Maureen wouldn't be pleased. There was already a small onshore reception party – Maureen, the nanny, two barking dogs and a goose – to hinder the last efforts of my saviour. By now, the front of the boat had lodged in the muddy patch where I'd torn away the grass, and the stern was being swept around with the current. Later, in the bath, I thought of the lost boot, being dragged along the bottom of the river and finally coming to rest, full of mud and gravel, somewhere near Henley.

There were low mutterings about how easy it was for a boy of four to fall from a tree growing out over the river and, amid professions of motherly love from Maureen, threats to have it removed. But nothing came of this resolve to punish nature for an unnatural carelessness on my part. I hated the thought of any alteration to my surroundings. In the meantime, the water had made a powerful claim on me, or so it felt. A claim which I still honour in dreams, as a fast-flowing river wrestles me down to a depth I can't measure, with a force I can't resist, bearing me into a world where the barriers between the enchanted space of my childhood and the unknown wilderness that lay beyond it have been overwhelmed by a fabulous flood.

Maureen, for her part, settled on the impossible project of keeping her boy away from the capricious force that surrounded us.

Our day had come. A clerk with a purple cardigan and big spectacles unlocked the door of court number 1. Ann Pike entered the empty courtroom. I followed her in. The clerk switched on a computer below the bench, picked up an audiotape and placed it in a tape deck. She went out through a door and returned with the court recorder just behind her. The court – all two of us – rose with due solemnity. The court recorder bowed. Her face wore a stern expression, the effect diminished somewhat by a generous matronly flapping around the hips as she made to sit down. Her voice was rather posh, and not unattractive.

She saw why we might have requested disclosure.

'But I would like reassurance that this won't cause distress to any member of the family – reassurance, that is to say, from you or from . . .'

'Mr Harding,' my adoption counsellor put in.

She turned to me: 'I shall address myself to your social worker, Mr Harding, but you may intervene at any time, if you wish.' And then to Ann: 'What of the adoptive parents in this case?'

It seemed proper to intervene, but what was I to say about Mother Two? How should her bleak indisposition be conveyed, across twenty feet of empty courtroom, to a woman of substance, kindly enough? Maureen, I said, was in an old people's home; she wasn't to know what was going on. The recorder looked at me as though I could indeed be the heartless sort. I went on to say that Colin, my adoptive father, was no longer alive. The word 'dead' might seem worse than heartless. My father, I said, and then something or other, and then 'deceased'.

'Deceased,' said the recorder with the mildest hint of contempt.

'Dead,' I said and she leaned back with a look of satisfaction, followed by a brisk, compassionate inclination of the neck.

We went quickly through the rest of the adoptive family, including Peter and Jill.

'Are they aware that you were adopted?'

'Yes, certainly.'

'And is it your understanding that they were always aware of that fact?'

No, they were not. Not in the beginning. In any case we saw each other so seldom. But sooner or later they were told, or they found out. They'd have known for thirty years or more, I said. The court recorder looked at me a little doubtfully.

'Miss Pike,' she said to Ann, 'I am happy for you to inspect the file, if you wish.'

This, she went on to tell us, Ann might do in her professional capacity, without jeopardising the confidentiality of the court, which – she was sure we'd understand – must be respected at all costs. It would be improper for me to have direct access. I was taken back.

It was a matter of discretion, Ann explained as we stepped out of the courtroom. She too had been surprised by the ruling. She'd felt the balance of opinion in the courts beginning to turn in favour of disclosure.

'It all depends if they're moving with the liberal current,' she remarked. Outside the building she pointed to a café over the road. 'Why don't you wait over there? I shouldn't be more than an hour.'

Each year, when the floods came and commuting daily to London grew too laborious for Colin, there was a weekly migration, a retreat to the flat in Notting Hill. Here Colin and Maureen took up provisional lives – everything was provisional – accompanied by their retinue: their little boy, part stranger, part accomplice; the nanny; two dogs, one cat; and occasionally, during the holidays, Peter or Jill. The memory of those Sunday afternoon departures, just before dark, is still vivid to me. Bread and scrapings were put out for the goose, which would have to make do until the following Friday. A pale mist hung like crêpe above the lawns at the front and back, now indistinguishable from the river; the lawn at the side of the house was also under water. The cottage itself, with its lightless windows, seemed to be afloat, like a votive leaf without a candle.

As I waited for Ann Pike in the café, I could restage the sensation of being removed from this fluid habitat to which, at times, I must have felt an almost umbilical connection, as if everything I needed were coursing directly into my system. Preparations for the uncoupling, repeated several times each winter – much less troubling once I'd been sent away to school – started early on Sunday morning. By the afternoon, Maureen had begun shouting at the nanny; the animals were in a state of low-level panic; and Colin, always smoking, had fallen into a defensive abstraction.

The journey to London was not without its horrors for Colin and Maureen, who hated the sight of growing conurbations for people unlike themselves. Slough was the one on which our route most often touched. And though it was a joke between them that if anybody misbehaved, the punishment would be 'a month in Slough', Colin and Maureen were filled with a humourless dread as we crawled past the industrial estates at the edge of the Great West Road. As I grew older, and still did the journey with them occasionally – by now along the M4 for much of the way – I realised that Slough embodied one of their deepest objections to post-war Britain: the growing proximity of the working classes to some of the better golf courses. The shadow of change, from which there might be no escape, always seemed to loom over them.

Ann had advised keeping notes about these intimate landscapes and people. I was a conscientious note-taker in my ordinary working life, but all I could think to note down in the little book I had open on the café table was the word 'Slough'.

For five days, an eternity in the life of a child, I would wither and skulk in town, getting under Maureen's feet when she was least inclined to be the loving mother, or I'd torment the nanny, a young woman given to bouts of homesickness for Germany. In spite of my liking for the riverside life, my sense of what was mine underwent another major extension at around this time. I was beginning to ease my sense of exile in London by annexing every inch of ground on the route between Notting Hill and our dens in the Thames Valley. The Great West Road – and much besides – was becoming mine as a matter of course. Even Slough had its special, disconsolate way of belonging to me.

In London, all the same, I longed for Friday and Colin's early appearance in the flat after a morning at the office, the loading of the Humber – a temperamental monster with wide running boards

– the rearranging of the dogs in the back seat and, finally, the capture of the cat and the slamming of doors that signalled our departure.

The smell of petrol and upholstery. Turning round and facing backwards to see the Lucozade advertisement. Then Slough, or by a diversion from the normal route, Staines ('a weekend in Staines' or 'a year in Timbuktu' were alternative punishments on offer from Colin).

Half an hour of daylight might have remained when we encountered the first floodwater. The car would be abandoned a few hundred yards from the course of the Loddon. The slow process of wading, fetching, carrying and returning then began, in a flurry of technicalities, arguments, remonstrations involving Colin, Maureen and the nanny. Boots the height of cowboys' chaps were put on, dogs shouldered, bottles of gin pocketed and food carried in plywood crates. A few minutes' strenuous wading from the car, there was a footbridge to the cottage, the lower planks covered by water. On the other side, in order to get from the bridge to the house, a dinghy was moored by a long painter to the last in a row of poplars running down one side of the submerged garden. If all was well, and the operation had gone smoothly, we would stumble over the bridge together – as a family, you could say.

Then the ritual crossing towards the cottage – the end of all the longing, as Colin set me down in the bow of the dinghy, still as an effigy, and helped Maureen into the middle of the boat. From here, she kept up a stream of lamentation as she ministered to the cat, both parties equally dismayed by boats and water, and indignantly sure that such things were beneath them. As indeed they were – though only the cat took in the full magnitude of that circumstance, clawing at Maureen's lambskin coat and wailing like an infant dangled over rapids. While Colin stood in the dinghy detaching the sodden rope from the poplar, Maureen would denounce the folly of their lives. Only Colin could subject her to such pointless hardship.

Colin slid the oars into the rowlocks and bent forward for the first stroke. The boat drew out from the trees and, as the cat's wailing and Maureen's blather seemed to die away behind me, we cut quickly through the idle floodwater that covered a swathe of the back garden. Often a grey mist hung in panels, veiling and revealing the remains of the afternoon light, and the cottage itself, with its dark, lifeless windows, drawing closer, fading again and reappearing closer still.

There was a roofed entranceway by the back garden, but alighting and unloading here was difficult. Colin always took the dinghy along the side of the cottage and down towards the river, where a faint drag from the current required more effort as he ferried us across what was, for most of the year, a long, crescent-shaped rose bed, and around to the front. On the wooden deck in front of the weathered double doors at this entrance to the cottage, our goose would be moping, surrounded by a slippery action painting in greys and greens, along with the scant remains of the food we'd laid out five days earlier. Colin brought the dinghy in towards the steps, accompanied by a frenzy of honking and clattering. As he did so, the cat would make a bid for terra firma, tearing itself out of Maureen's arms, leaping from my shoulder to the deck, skidding across the moraine of goose-shit with the goose in pursuit and performing a final leap for the window ledge beside the doors. Meanwhile Colin drew the stern around so that Maureen could mount the steps without calamity. Then me behind her, very quickly, abandoning the nanny. Then the dogs. And Colin, for once resigned, happy perhaps to be alone in the boat for a few seconds.

I could find nothing in all this worth entering in my nearly empty notebook, perhaps because I'd always been able to see us in that disembarkation, flailing and obtuse, every brute for itself, resolute if not happy.

The cottage was raised on several feet of brickwork – there'd been flooding in these parts for years. Only once had the water risen above the height of the brick and damaged the carpets and floors – and that was back in some legendary time that didn't count. But whenever the waters were high, a miasma seemed to rise through the floors of the cottage, infecting everything with the smell of mud and live bait. Moving from room to room, you could feel it parting like fetid drapery, and so, on our arrival, Maureen and Colin would busy themselves with the electricity supply, hot water bottles for the beds, oil stoves for the kitchen and living room, and it wasn't long before the damp that had inveigled its way into every crevice of the house during our absence was smothered by a fug of burning paraffin.

Ann had taken detailed notes on the court file. She was getting them out of her bag as she came through the door of the café. She'd been right to think that there might not be much to go on. The London County Council report on the adoption stated the facts of the case succinctly. The boy was the 'illegitimate son of an unmarried woman'. The applicants for adoption had assumed 'care and custody' of the child in July 1952. And then – a surprise this – the arrangements for adoption were 'made by a third party'. It had indeed been organised outside the normal channels – the adoption agencies, churches and charitable organisations for unmarried mothers – and had come directly under the supervision of the local authority. Another surprise: the counter assistant at 'Chain Stores' gave her boy away after eleven days – Maureen had always said three. Once custody had passed to Colin and Maureen, there had been meetings with a child welfare officer and then a child protection visitor. The situation was satisfactory. By the summer of 1953, when the adoption was legalised, the child welfare officer reported to the court that the boy was receiving 'good care' and had been baptised.

But there was a complication, to do with Maureen's earlier marriage, from which Colin had removed her abruptly in 1950, and in particular with Maureen's two children by her first husband. A remark in the County Council report explained why the court recorder might have withheld the file – and why she might have thought to tell Ann to use her own judgment in the matter: 'It is understood that the two children regard the infant as their natural brother and that the whole family are not aware of the adoption. It is not clear whether they will be told the exact situation later on.'

But with Peter and Jill now in their sixties, it would have been odd to deny me access on these grounds. Perhaps the court recorder was a firm believer in 'closed adoption'.

The name of the family doctor was given – the one who'd found the ducks in Mim's bed – and the name of Colin and Maureen's referee. Both were now dead. There was the briefest résumé of Maureen's adult life: 'divorced, two children, TB; treatment for 12 years.' (She used to cite tuberculosis as the reason why she couldn't give birth to a third child.) There was the fact that Colin's parents let him and Maureen live rent-free in the flat in Notting Hill. Apparently his earnings as a stockbroker in 1952 amounted to £1,200.

The only really new information took the form of a name: 'Mrs Privett of Ladbroke Grove'. Mrs Privett was the third party who had arranged the adoption. She was down in the notes as 'Mrs Harding's ex-char lady'.

'Assuming you decide to take this further,' Ann said in the café, 'that name might unlock a door. If she's alive, which is possible, she could be fairly easy to find. You won't come across many Privetts in the phone book or the electoral registers, but I'm afraid there are plenty of Margaret Walshes.'

There was one other thing – an observation made by the child welfare officer about Margaret Walsh in his written remarks for the finalisation procedure in July 1953: 'At the time of reporting, it has not proved practicable to interview the mother personally. She does not appear very co-operative but efforts are still being made to contact her and the result will be reported verbally to the Court.'

Ann and I parted company outside the café. There was no reason for us to meet again and I was in low spirits for a day or so.

By the time Maureen let it be known that I was not quite her son, and all the more hers for that, we were living in the most eccentric of our places by the river – a houseboat, a few hundred yards from Rosemary Cottage and away from the Loddon. The tutelary river was now the Thames: the two watercourses were a little further apart here than at the cottage.

The houseboat was about fifty or sixty feet by twenty, an ungainly vessel with five rooms, a walkway running around its sides and an exterior stairway leading to a flat roof. There was a white handrail the length of the walkway and another enclosing the roof. Everything was white, apart from the roof itself, which was spread with pitch, and the hull. The boat had been brought up on to dry land several years before we began living in it. It was an easy craft for a child to commandeer. The river was hard by. There were long, imagined reaches in need of exploration, complicated passageways overhung by weeping willow, beech trees and small oaks wound with ivy, which strained out over the water. I was kept busy.

Maureen was not a devotee of the houseboat. She complained of the damp, even in warm weather, and was worried that sooner or later I would slip off the roof. No longer death by drowning for her boy, but death by falling, as a bright, gesticulating shape flashed past the window of the so-called kitchen and landed with a perfunctory squelch.

On summer evenings, Maureen and Colin would sit in the largest room, at the centre of the boat, with their backs to the Thames and the double doors open, like colonials in charge of an obscure up-country station, relaxing after a long day's duty. The ground on which they looked out ran flat for about thirty yards and ended in a prolific screen of foliage – willow and hawthorn mostly, fed by a dip in the ground. This was the best view from the houseboat, away from the river and on to the area that Colin, a patient gardener, would slowly transform over several years and lovingly restore in the spring after the floods had done their worst.

Those evenings of light and well-being on a rotting boat at the edge of a well-tended garden – a boat that would have sunk within minutes of being returned to the water – perfectly expressed the odd condition of our ménage: Colin, Maureen and me, and our gaggle of pets and servants, in that order. By virtue of our living on a boat, we were to my way of thinking always adrift. Truer, probably, to think of us as beached – a condition a bit like the moated life that promised peace and quiet. Although on the face of it we were unusual, nothing unusual ever happened to us. Summer was an unending succession of days without mishap.

Colin and Maureen had grand names for ordinary things. Just as the rectangle of grass at the back of the cottage was 'the tennis court', so the deck built out from the main doors of the houseboat, which you reached by a set of wooden steps, was known as 'the veranda'. The piles of brick on which the boat itself was raised were 'columns' and the row of sleepers set on two stout joists over the ditch we had to cross to reach the property became 'the small bridge'. The houseboat itself, equipped with a generator and running water pumped from a well, but otherwise poorly appointed, was called *Nirvana*. The Buddhist state of enlightenment. It was only later that these entanglements of makeshift and exoticism struck me as comic.

Maureen's stories about her earlier life were part of the rich improbability of our world. They were drawn from a store of fantasies not unlike my own. While she spent her time embroidering the daydream of an earlier, more splendid existence, with horse-drawn carriages and large houses, I was happy enough in the pursuit of adventure on and around the houseboat. It was a good arrangement.

I can't put a time to it. It seems, in my mind, to have been the summer after I fell in the Loddon. In any case, it was a warm evening. Maureen sat me down in the main room of the houseboat and explained that the word for a child with no parents was 'orphan'. She was an orphan herself, she told me, and she had been brought up by her grandmother. She said nothing about her parents dying, and I understood only that she'd been unable to stay with these people, whoever they were.

Did I know, she went on, that I was a bit like her – a bit like an orphan?

No.

But I wasn't really an orphan; I was *like* an orphan. (Possibly a little amphibious creature, a young boy might have thought, part dwarf, part dolphin.) When I was born, Maureen explained, I was extremely small and it was around that time, or that size, in my life that Colin had paid a visit to the hospital. Afterwards, the three of us had lived happily. A double happiness that was somehow threefold: Colin and Maureen were happy that he had gone to the hospital; and I was happy, surely, as a result of his doing so.

Maureen used the word 'adopted' – I imagine her saying, 'You're what I call adopted' – and asked me to say it with her. I don't think she mentioned anything about another mother in this, the first telling. Not long after our conversation, Colin appeared at the far end of the garden, having walked the ten minutes from the village railway station. He stepped through a diminutive wrought-iron gateway nearly overrun by brambles and known as 'the main gate'. Quite possibly I thought he had been to the hospital again to prepare for another arrival.

Yet nothing that Maureen had said seemed odd. She was my mother, and a generous mother, and descriptions of the kind she gave came easily – naturally, you'd say – in those days. They spoke eloquently, urgently, of the world as she saw it, and to a child, the way a mother sees a thing is mostly how it is. I recall being intrigued by our talk – slightly restless, I suppose. And in that memory, which is only partly to be trusted, the evening sun shines through the back window of the main room; the roof of the houseboat beckons.

She must have told her tale with delicacy. It was persuasive and straightforward and led me to conclude that all children were simply dispensed from a hospital. (I recall tiffs at school, before I'd reached the age of six, about how babies arrived in families: I was sure that the tummy story was playground obscurantism.) Then, some time afterwards, at an inopportune moment when the weather was fine and there was a lot going on outside, the parents sat their children down, described the comings and goings from hospital and coached them in the mastery of a new word: 'adopted'.

I continued to wonder in a cursory way whether Colin had plans to bring home more children, and at the next telling, perhaps a few months later, when Maureen introduced the character of the little girl in London who'd given me up, my thoughts prowled across the water and established a tenuous link with the unfamiliar world in which I imagined her. But Maureen's own potted autobiography was in many ways the star turn of these little talks and it gripped me. Her grandmother had taken her to Egypt (where was that? Was it in London?); pyramids (what were they?) towered above the desert (but what was that?). There was a stone animal, the 'sphinx', which I took for a long time to be a pair of something, such as slippers or scissors. Time had elapsed. Slowly? Quickly? I can't say. At some point, Maureen and her grandmother had returned to England to live in a big house – but how big? Bigger than Rosemary Cottage or the houseboat, or the flat in London. Bigger than all of them put together. Maureen's grandmother had a horse-drawn carriage, driven by a coachman. Maureen used to ride in it, and the Dalmatians kept by the old lady – 'Dalmatians?' 'Spotted dogs' – would trot behind.

Had I been older, I'd have thought of Maureen as an eligible young lady in an early nineteenth-century novel, pale and presentable, with witty conversation and a range of accomplishments. But her story took place some time in the 1920s, about a hundred years too late. Now and then, or was it once, she went skittering over snow and ice in a cold place called Chamonix, definitely near London.

Yet in the unfolding of this family origin myth, with its puzzles and enigmas, my own provenance and Maureen's background were endowed with a fantastic, deceptive clarity. It was clear to me that adoption was the way all children came into their families. Very likely their mothers had all been to 'Egypt' and surged up long gravel driveways in a jingling coach and four with Dalmatians bringing up the rear, sometimes in ice and snow.

What I couldn't explain, subsequently, was my willingness to say nothing about the story of my coming about to Colin's parents and his sister – and if the court records are correct, to the young Peter and Jill as well. I tried to remember when the small boy had first been advised that what he knew about his arrival in the world was something he should keep to himself. Was it soon after the first telling – the 'broaching', as I thought of it – or did it happen at the same time? Either way, he seemed to have taken it on, but swept away all trace of having received the instruction, like a spy swallowing the bit of paper containing the coded message. What if he'd divulged the secret? Would the world have turned to dust?

A flash of identification, clear and articulate at first, but growing blurred, as though you'd seen someone you knew in a crowd and then lost track of them. 'At the time of reporting, it has not proved practicable to interview the mother personally.' Imagine a very young woman refusing to confirm her original decision or to commit another signature to paper. 'She does not appear very co-operative.'

A straight back outlined in a light summer coat disappears round a corner; the same woman in the same coat kills time at a relative's flat while the visitor from the Child Welfare Department calls at her own flat and finds no one there.

All I'd needed to trigger this little hallucination was a couple of sentences in a report. Blood may lead people to search for one another, to know more about the tribe, but it has little to add to the work of the imagination, which begins every time we hear about strangers in difficulty, or pass a war memorial. I'd already come to think of the child welfare officer as the writer of Margaret Walsh's secret epitaph – an epitaph held on file by the courts. I didn't like it because it explained nothing about her impatience with the entourage of law enforcers and welfare workers who wouldn't let her be. If she hadn't minded giving up the child, they would have struck her as a nuisance. But if she had, they could only compound her dismay. Her reluctance to 'co-operate' was nonetheless the most intimate thing I'd heard about her, and for that reason I clung to it. And already I found myself taking her side.

The moment had come to draft the opening lines of a tribute to Margaret. I made a short entry in a computer file, about a hundred words in all. The following day, a Saturday, I drove out along the Westway without quite knowing what I had in mind. I passed St Mary's Paddington on my left – the hospital where Maureen had said I was born. Cairo, Chamonix, Paddington, anywhere was possible with Maureen. I could make nothing of it.

I drove around the White City Estate but didn't get out of the car. I felt odd in the head, confused. I cut south and worked my way back to Notting Hill via Shepherds Bush. I tried to remember why, as a boy, I'd felt uneasy about London and preferred the wetter margins of my world. I spoke Margaret's name out loud in the car and then put on the radio. I drove around aimlessly for a time and pulled into a residents' parking space near the crest of Ladbroke Grove. I got out of the car and smoked, and thought some more about the old uneasiness with London. It didn't seem to be connected with adoption. More to do with Colin and Maureen's own anxieties about the city, Maureen's particularly, for the only way they could deal with it was as a domain, like our domain by the river. They'd hoped to customise it, carving out a proprietorial fantasy, as childish as mine, that set them against the grain of the city, which had its own democratic insistence on how life should be lived. Theirs was an absolute faith in privacy, but not the negotiated privacy that a city proposes. They liked to be free of any exchange, whether it was paying rates or travelling too often on trains and buses, that would involve them, however remotely, with the public nature of London. They had an almost fawning devotion to the idea of exclusiveness. They liked clubs and restaurants that were hard to get into. They talked more often about certain friends than others: usually the grander ones, and very often the richer ones. The shape they'd hoped to give the city involved them in precarious bouts of social climbing that did them no justice and, in trying to keep up with the people they wished to cultivate, cost them larger and larger sums of money. It must have been exhausting. It was unlike anything that London had come to mean to me.

I knew the city better now and liked it a great deal. And, as I did when I'd heard about her early on, I imagined Margaret – dead or alive – to be out there somewhere, in that enormity, lost from view in the vast open-endedness from which Colin and Maureen recoiled, presenting my adoption as a rescue operation from a menacing, overpowering place. I suppose it *was* a rescue operation, but at times it could seem like an abduction, which took me away from an ordinary life, with ordinary footholds in the world, into a fantasy of their devising.

I went around on to Holland Park Avenue, north off the roundabout at Shepherds Bush and rejoined the Westway back into town. I took up a respectable position in the long tailback from the first set of lights on the Marylebone Road and wallowed happily behind the windscreen wipers. I'd have preferred it if the birth certificate had named the father in column four. There would have been another lead, another way to go. The chances of fingering a Father One were slim.

Did paternity matter?

The answer took the form of a question.

Did you love Colin?

Yes. But I knew him. He was my friend and protector and I was his little boy. The Scandinavian sailor was another matter.

I nudged the car forward, wondering more directly about Margaret Walsh and where on earth she'd ended up.

I told myself that if I could come off the ramp on to Marylebone Road before the traffic lights at the bottom changed, it would be a sign she'd been living somewhere in London at the time of her death.

I was off and through the lights and that was one mystery out of the way.

The part of me that was sure Margaret Walsh was dead had to struggle with her recent acquisition of a name, which seemed at times to make her death less likely. But almost every dead person had a name and Margaret Walsh might simply be a string of animated syllables that would turn up again at the end of a long search as an inscription in a cemetery. Or more likely an entry in the Register of Births, Marriages and Deaths. Sooner or later, I reckoned, I'd be looking for her in 'Deaths'. But first I'd have to establish the new surname she'd probably taken some time after I was born, since in all likelihood she had gone on to marry.

*

Mrs Privett would remain a name on paper, I supposed. The way she'd been described said more about Maureen than it did about her. Ex or otherwise, 'char lady' was a fine expression, with its injunction to the lower orders to assume their proper place in life. Maureen used it often. Yet the longer I thought about it, the harder it got to fix her sense of working people. She might just as well have hated the expression char lady and told off other people for using it.

As time had gone on, the rules governing her usage had become more mysterious to me; so had her notions of etiquette. And then, instead of liking her as a boy likes his mother, I began to like her for her oddity, and the difficulty of predicting what she might say. In this, her drinking was an asset: it spiced things up, and before it began to tell on her terribly, she was a slightly dangerous person to be with.

At the same time, she had a gracious way of putting those whom Colin thought beneath us perfectly at their ease, and in doing so, she too was clearly more relaxed than she sometimes seemed. Hours were spent nattering gaily with cleaning ladies or repairmen. But from this rich, hospitable soil, intransigent opinions could suddenly erupt.

'What they need', I heard her say many times about workers in dispute, whose union leaders might crop up on the news, 'is the biggest dose of unemployment . . .'

And then it would tail off.

In fact, her politics were non-existent, which is to say mild, and I'm not sure she knew what a trade union was. She might have said, for instance, 'It's what I call a trade union.'

At the time of the first 1974 election – my visits were by then extremely rare – she announced with dismay that the 'socialists' would shortly be in power.

Well into her evening refreshments already, she had assembled her band of pedigree dogs by the sofa: two or three toy Pekinese and a minuscule Yorkshire terrier, to which she'd given strangely raffish names. Bertie, Porchy, Suki and another I can't repeat. They were about as far as you could stray from a Dalmatian while bearing the

word 'dog' in mind. And bad advertisements, like the court paint-
ings of Velazquez, for the effects of narrow breeding. The Pekinese,
in which the central feature of the stove-in nose was prized, had
been refined with so little thought for their oxygen supply that even
the hardest heart would flutter with pity to hear them squeak and
snort from one breath to the next, like rubber ducks plunged to the
bottom of a bubble bath and squeezed a bit at a time.

'Yes, darling,' said Maureen. 'We've come to the end of our –
well, you know how your father hates Labour, and I hate, I agree
I suppose, if they're going to do *that*, then it *is* the end. Which I'm
sure they will! Horrible!'

I wasn't clear what the Labour Party had in mind for her.

'You don't understand,' she said, unable to restrain the first
tears of exasperation. 'You're so *stupid*! I wouldn't mind if it was
us they took away. But it's the doggies they want to take. Can't
you see that?'

And now she was in crying in earnest.

'Why would any government want them,' I asked after a long
interval in the conversation, 'when they smell so terribly?'

She appeared to rally.

'I love them, don't I, Porchy?' – blowing her nose and attending
bravely to her face. 'You may not think it's possible to love a dog-
gie but we do. And anyway it's nonsense that they smell.' She
fixed me with her dwindling blue eyes. 'When did *you* last have a
bath is what Porchy wants to know.'

We sat in silence, a little embarrassed, deferring to the television.
The pets snuffled and gasped on the carpet.

'Have a drink, darling,' she said at last, smoothing down her
dress. And as I stood up: 'I think I'll have a top-up myself . . .'

'It's in *Black August*,' she went on, still thinking of the dogs. 'It's
a terrifying book. A . . .' – always the slight pause before the
heights of the sentence – '. . . prophecy.' And then, apologetically,
without quite conceding defeat: 'I don't know. I'm not a clever
woman. It's by whatsisname, your father plays golf with him, he
did *The Devil Rides Out*.'

She was thinking of Dennis Wheatley. *Black August*, she

explained, was about a vicious plebeian uprising that took its toll on the better neighbourhoods. And no doubt the better class of pet.

Much of Maureen's life was spent in this squeamish, embattled frame of mind. Yet the next thing you knew, she was out on the town with her hairdresser, or entertaining the cleaning lady or the decorator with a complicated cocktail and then a refresher. Or she'd be away on a pub-crawl with people her husband had never heard of. If she'd lived by an industrial estate, she'd soon have found friends from the shop floors and warehouses, but like children who gulp down milk but shy away from cows, our family kept as far as we could from the sources of the many things on which we depended.

'I like *people*,' Maureen used to say when Colin reprimanded her for seeing this person or that person. 'You're a snob and I'm not.'

It was true that Maureen liked people, and it was this, more than her love of very small dogs, that accounted for much of her charm.

In those days, the name 'Mrs Privett' might have rung a bell with Maureen. 'Mrs Privett of Ladbroke Grove' – the only useful name in the adoption file. Still, I wasn't sure. Maureen had had plenty of staff over the years and it would have been typical of her not to remember the cleaner who'd known a poor girl with a troublesome pregnancy.

Now, in any case, there was no sense to be got from her. She had lost her mind. The chances of a proper conversation were far less than they'd been on that memorable election day when she'd mustered her pets around the sofa and wept.

After Colin's death in 1991, Maureen had gone into sheltered accommodation – an attractive, expensive block of flats off Holland Park Avenue. There she'd taken to drink in a big way, bigger than ever before. She'd scarcely settled in when Jill came up to London.

Jill and Maureen were by now very much alike.

Jill had been a stubby girl with pigtails, a sweet, bemused sort of person. When she wasn't at boarding school or off at her father's, she'd spent her time at riding school or gymkhanas. She'd been mad about horses and later about teenage boys, especially boys with a propensity to bolt.

I knew her no better, possibly less well, than I knew our nannies – after the German nanny came the Swiss one, and after her the French one – but by the time I'd grown up, things had turned out badly for Jill, and when she started coming to London to see Maureen in the first stages of her decline, she too was flailing at the edge of her own undoing. She'd become as slight and haggard as her mother, with the same mannerisms, the same blonde hair – though Maureen's was greyer and thinner since Colin's death – and the same way of taking pleasure to desolate extremes. Both were now known for extravagant feats of bad behaviour after a drink or two, which is how they entertained one another on Jill's visits, returning in due course to the flats in Maureen's new residence, ringing every bell on the console and subjecting the staff to what was later described as 'racial abuse'.

A few weeks after the management had issued a stern warning, I was summoned by a nurse on duty at the flats. Maureen had been missing most of the day.

'I'm afraid your sister's decided to visit again,' the nurse said over the phone. She spoke with an air of foreboding that none the less suggested the worst was already under way.

Maybe I should threaten to disown Maureen and Jill, I thought as I got into the car. Possibly shout and wave my arms at them in a show of consternation. But by now there were no real family ties to revoke. Should I shout and wave my arms anyway?

Driving west along Notting Hill Gate, I thought I saw Maureen and Jill. I stopped the car on a yellow line. No doubt about it at this range. Like a spent, delirious swimmer who's crawled up the beach to the wrong bathing hut, Jill was hammering on the glass door of a restaurant while the waiters rapidly secured it from the inside. Maureen, meanwhile, was sitting on the pavement with her shoes off, legs stretched out over the kerb, as though she were lounging on the sands at Deauville. It was nine at night. The traffic was humming down to Shepherds Bush. Moat-people fetch up in unlikely places.

After that, Maureen had been moved on. She was now two establishments further afield, well out of London and harm's way. We'd last spoken in the middle of the night, when she was still allowed to keep a dog, a neurotic miniature in the same style as the others. She'd called me to say that she'd packed a suitcase for him – I knew immediately she meant the dog – but she couldn't recall the way to his school. 'He's a sweet chap but he can't sit here with me all day, not now the holidays are over. Is that unreasonable of me?'

'Are you sure you're not thinking of Jeremy?' I asked.

'Yes, of course. D'you take me for a fool?'

'No, but this is . . . You're on the phone to Jeremy now.'

'Don't be ridiculous. Who?'

'You've muddled me up with your dog,' I went on, 'and it's gone two in the morning.'

'I'm so sorry.' She sounded mortified. 'I had no idea it was so late. Now just remind me who this is again, and I'll have one of the staff here ring you back.'

The following morning she called again. Was I in a position to cover the cost of little fellow's education? 'Just this term, anyhow, until we're sorted out and we've talked to the bank.'

'Consider it covered,' I said.

'Oh thank you, darling,' she said with a sigh of relief. 'He's such a lucky boy.'

IV

Characters

It's one of the axioms of adoption that when you go looking for
people you don't know, you begin to discover the people you imagined you knew.

With Maureen very much out of the running, there was only one
other person I could think of to see, this side of the adoption firewall. My aunt Rosemary, Colin's sister, was a charming old lady.
She had always been good to me. Indeed, she'd become a sort of
benefactor, and a living link to the memory of her mother Mim – my
grandmother by my account – in a way that Colin, so often at odds
with everyone, could never really be. Not that Rosemary would
have known about Mrs Privett of Ladbroke Grove, or any of this.
On the contrary, I hadn't been meant to breathe a word of it to her.
But she may have guessed. And if so, it was admirable of her never
to raise it with me. The 'issue', as they say, was my business, and if
she knew about it, she chose not to have it out in the open. That left
me with a troubled conscience, and I acted on it, in the belief she
should know I was taking an interest in Margaret Walsh.

We'd corresponded often, and I visited her from time to time.
She too was in an old people's home, but in rather better shape
than Maureen – the machinery of excavation was still in working
order. In Maureen's case everything had creaked to a halt: you
had to put your ear to the ground to hear flurries of rubble clattering in the condemned shafts or a muffled detonation deep in the
seam, and then give an encouraging nod of the head – up and
down, sideways, it didn't much matter.

I mentioned the adoption to Rosemary in a letter, almost in
passing, and went down to see her a week or so later. She was my
only remaining connection with that part of the world. 'What I call
the Thames Valley,' Maureen used to say; nowadays I thought of it
as 'floodland', a trick I used to protect the vivid landscapes of my

childhood from any association with the nearby villages, whose names would only lure me away into memories of adolescence.

Rosemary was always keen for us to visit. She enjoyed the fact that her nephew was married and liked to see her clutch of great-nephews from time to time. She'd done without marriage and children of her own, but was pleased to monitor the progress of a young family at a comfortable distance, on her own territory. It was always understood that when we visited her, we should come as a full expeditionary force: mother and father, carload of child-paraphernalia and finally the 2.4 children themselves.

We sat in a country pub a few hundred yards from the old people's home and went most of the meal without raising the subject at all. Then, over dessert, while the children were out in the garden, playing by the four-wheel drives, Rosemary announced briskly that my letter hadn't surprised her in the least.

She was tucking into an ice-cream with a complicated flavour. She was a small person, like Colin, with the same small mouth, given to momentous utterances between birdlike mouthfuls, delivered in a matter-of-fact way, from which she'd rapidly seek to indemnify you in case of injury with a cascade of small talk.

'Do you remember when you were seventeen,' she said, 'and you had a frightful row with your parents? You came over to see Mim and me, and you told us you couldn't go home, and we put you up for the summer. And if I remember correctly, you said that in the heat of the moment Maureen had told you she'd got you from the gutter?'

All of this vouched for the accuracy of my aunt's memory – perfectly true.

'Maureen does say shocking things now and then,' she went on, 'but I'm unshockable, as you know, and I was more perplexed than anything. Your grandmother and I spoke a little about it later. She didn't seem troubled. She said something like: "I don't care where they got him from. He's my grandson." Anyway, we never had any proof, and we never wanted any. It was all the same to us. You were Colin and Maureen's child – and I'm still your ancient aunt.'

43

She laughed her high-pitched laugh, which always made her eyes water.

'You see, the thing was,' Rosemary said, 'Maureen never wanted another child. That was my firm impression. She'd had the two by the first marriage and then she ran off with Colin. Well, naturally, with this being his first marriage, he did – he was keen to have a son – but she put up stiff resistance. We could all see that. Mim was fearfully upset. And then there was the business of Maureen's TB – you knew about that, didn't you? It wasn't supposed to be safe for her to have another. I remember her saying so. I don't suppose she wanted any more children by any means, and if you ask me, an adopted child was no better, from her point of view, than the real thing.'

'No,' I said. 'I see that.'

I thought: 'Good care.' Maureen's reluctance to go for another child merely confirmed what a dutiful parent she'd been to her unwished-for boy. Heroic, possibly, that she never let on.

'Of course,' Rosemary added, 'she came to love you. These things probably take time, and anyway she wasn't a monster.'

'No one thought of her as a monster,' I said, losing track of our lunch for a few seconds and drifting towards Maureen's bed in the old people's home, like the prince who means to bring his princess back from oblivion. I prop her up and shake her gently by the shoulder. She looks at me and then at the abyss behind me. I kiss her on both cheeks. It's me, I say, it's not one of the dogs.

That's right, she says, it's you.

The gin is on the sideboard. There's tonic in the fridge.

Here's to Mother Two, I say.

And here's to you, darling.

'Quite,' said Rosemary, dabbing her mouth with a yellow paper napkin and pushing away the remains of her ice-cream.

And what of the gutter? I wondered. It was not quite out of Maureen's top drawer, as in 'the biggest dose of unemployment'; just a curious bit of class animosity that came from nowhere.

The waitress was approaching with two espresso-sized cups filled with instant coffee, giving off the faint but unmistakable smell of Marmite.

'My little relatives are splendid,' Rosemary announced, reaching for her napkin again and peering out at the figures in the garden as though she were surveying Nova Scotia from 35,000 feet.

Reg Christie's legacy was to have done away with a small part of the Ladbroke Grove area. The crimes were too awful and not long after Christie was hanged in 1953, Rillington Place was renamed Ruston Close: this might, among other things, deter the growing numbers of ghoulish sightseers. As the opportunities for redevelopment in the area increased, Ruston Close moved up the list. Some of the houses were boarded up in the early 1970s, with the construction of the Westway, but it was a few more years before the street was demolished.

On returning to the neighbourhood, I found the thought that the house had gone unsettling. It left a hole in my mental map and forced me back on the clutter in my head: Tommy Brock the badger, and his sackful of baby rabbits, making his way up Bull Banks to Mr Tod's house. He breaks in, puts the sack in the oven without bothering to light it, or even kill the rabbits, and sets the table. Then he snoozes in Mr Tod's bed. When Colin read me this story in the flat in Notting Hill, we used to linger over the colour plate showing Tommy Brock in bed with his boots on. Mr Tod is peering around the door.

Tommy Brock was described by Beatrix Potter as a 'disagreeable' character, but you'd have had to say something stronger about Christie. The same year that Margaret Walsh gave birth to her boy and informed the registrar she was living in Chesterton Road, Christie murdered his wife in his flat. It transpired that he'd killed other women before, and others shortly afterwards. Three years earlier, he'd offered to perform an abortion for Beryl Evans, the young mother who lived in the flat upstairs, when she'd got pregnant again, not long after the birth of her first child Geraldine. Abortion was illegal at the time but back-street methods offered an obvious way out of unwanted pregnancies. When the bodies of Beryl and Geraldine were discovered in the wash-house at the end of the garden, and suspicion fell on Beryl's husband Timothy, it

45

was Christie's evidence – and his quiet, impressive delivery – that put his neighbour in the way of the gallows.

In the preamble to Christie's own trial in 1953, it turned out that he'd kept an entourage of murdered women. Two had been buried in the garden years earlier. Three had been hastily stashed in his pantry after the despatch of his wife. And of course there was the wearisome Mrs Ethel Christie herself, whom he'd put under the floorboards. He confessed to killing Beryl Evans, but never to the murder of little Geraldine.

The grim celebrity of the street had lingered on, despite the change of name to Ruston Close. Demolition had been the only way forward. If you tried to find it now, the nearest you'd get would be Bartle Road, a redbrick development set back from an old Metropolitan Line viaduct.

Coming away from that viaduct and back on to Ladbroke Grove, I realised how close I was to another piece of the past that perhaps I'd been looking for without knowing it. When I got home, I rang directory enquiries and gave the name of an old friend of Colin's. Yes. And the address of the subscriber? Bassett Road, a few blocks north of Bartle Road. About an hour later I rang the number.

I hadn't seen my uncle Boris for years. I say 'my uncle', but this – like many of the kinships in my family – is an exaggeration. I knew this outspoken, clever man as Buncle Oris and he may have been my godfather. He came in and out of my early childhood with a reassuring regularity – in London especially, but there were also visits to floodland, where he spent Christmas with us more than once.

Colin and Boris met because they were good at cards. Well after they became friends, Colin drew up the official rules of Canasta, a new and fashionable game during the 1950s, and won the first international title, partnering up with a chancer by the name of Terence Reese. His passion, though, was bridge, and so was Boris's. They had remained friends through the 1960s and 1970s, but as Boris's career recovered from a cheating scandal – Reese was the partner – and he went from one success to another, Colin settled into a rut: a stylish, profitable rut no doubt, but he ceased

to cut such an impressive figure in the world on which he depended for a good deal of his income. The two men saw, and thought,
much less of one another.

'Your father's game was terrible,' Boris shouted, as he and his
wife – much the younger of the two – showed me into the living
room a bit before noon.

'Really, Boris,' she protested, 'I don't think he's interested in the
details of Colin's game.'

The flat was jumbled, not exactly untidy. Boris wore a silk
dressing gown and pampered an off-white poodle, a miniature
with purple tear stains under its eyes. I found him hardly
changed, though he wasn't far off ninety. The tremendous alertness and ruthless good humour were there, in perfect working
order, even if the body was a little fragile and the irreverent lustre
in the eyes a little dulled. And because he seemed to have
emerged straight from my childhood, I felt the glow of the early
Christmases with Colin and Maureen, the sense of unmanageable
happiness, like the happiness of a love affair. The first serious
swear word I heard, I remembered now, had come from Boris's
lips, carved into the gaiety of a New Year's Eve in floodland, and
delivered in the diamantine accent which went with the trim
moustache. (And isn't that Maureen, laughing affectionately, sip-
ping at a champagne cocktail?)

As I put my case, Boris's eyelids sagged with an air of indifference.
From time to time, there was a convulsive arching of the eyebrows.

'I simply don't see why you're bothering with this,' he said
when I'd done. 'But I'm delighted to help you, dear boy.'

He went on to speak in such detail about Colin and Maureen,
about our little trio, about Maureen's first marriage, about aunts I
barely remembered, and people of whom I had no recollection,
that for a moment Margaret Walsh began to look like a tremendous distraction. Wasn't Boris heading up the only respectable
inquiry – into the family I thought I'd known but hadn't?

In any case, he thought it silly and tasteless to go about looking
for your natural mother – and part of me was inclined to agree. In
the end, this kind of thing was both insufficiently serious and

insufficiently amusing – another part of me agreed.

Boris would have said that you got where you could as best you could. You walked at a steady, invigorating pace in the amplitude of your own life, like a big man enjoying a day in the country. You did well by the people you liked and you spread infamies about those you didn't care for. If you looked over your shoulder, you did so with a dismissive snort and a sense that you'd been lucky. In a contemptible world, there was very little worth dwelling on. Part of me consented to all this; and it was plain enough how Boris – whose family had fled the Bolsheviks and later been forced to close their offices in Germany because of the Nazis – came to see things the way he did.

He'd encountered Colin, he told me, not long after he'd arrived in Britain in the 1930s. They'd met at Crockford's – I remembered sitting in Crockford's as a little boy, needling the barman for maraschino cherries while Maureen had a few gins and we hung about until Colin was done.

'Your father,' said Boris, petting the poodle, 'was a bridge bum. When I met him, that is. He didn't work. He played bridge to make money, and he did so for some time. He meant to try his luck as a barrister, but the war got in the way of that.'

By the time he was demobilised – he'd have been in his early thirties – Colin had decided it would take too long to build a career at the bar, and he went back to the bridge tables.

'Eventually,' said Boris, 'I introduced him to a broker and he took a job in the City. But even once he was working, he didn't earn a lot, and he was always on the lookout for money from his family. And I suppose that's where you came in.'

His legs rearranged themselves with elderly enthusiasm under the silk dressing gown and then he sat back, looking me up and down.

'Well, Colin had an aunt you may not remember, called Phyllis . . . she'd have been your great-aunt, your grandfather's sister. But wait, dear boy . . . Let me get you some more coffee.'

He yelled out for his wife, a nickname that was hard to decipher, though distinctly French.

Boris spoke a lot of languages. And he knew every bidding convention in contract bridge.

'Oughtn't I to go back a bit?' he asked, suavely pleased with the little cliff-hanger he'd just set up. 'I'm thinking of Maureen's part of the story. It will fill out the picture. We don't want to get ahead of ourselves.'

'That's right,' I said, without much stomach for it: if we dug too far down, we might never get back to where I wanted to be. Where was that?

'Colin and I', he began, 'knew a man by the name of Graham, a good bridge player, and someone I saw quite a bit in the old days. He captained several teams, including the England team, at the major tournaments, and after he'd picked Colin for one of these events – I hasten to add he'd picked me before he picked your father – they became friends. We were all friends, I suppose. You may not remember Graham, but he was Maureen's first husband, Peter and Jill's father . . . you do, that's good. They were Surrey people; they had a grand house in Caterham. Graham was a rich fellow, talented, energetic, generous; he'd made most of his money as a printer – he published the daily Stock Exchange figures. Well, the story goes like this. I was invited to Caterham for a weekend. I went down on my own and early on the Sunday morning I got up, looked out of the window and saw Graham setting off in his car – one of his cars, I should say. I think he was driving a guest to the railway station. Then I saw him come back. About ten minutes went by and the next thing I knew he came bursting into my room to announce that he'd found Colin in bed with his wife. A servant had brought me the Sunday papers and I browsed a bit fitfully, I must confess, waiting for the twelve-bore to go off in the billiard room, but it didn't. Then, when I thought the coast was clear, I went down to breakfast. There they were at the table, Graham, Maureen and Colin, tucking into the kidneys and scrambled eggs as if nothing had happened.'

Boris's eyelids were fully raised and his eyes were brilliant with mischief – a thrilling mischief, I thought.

'Interesting, you'd have to agree. But let's come back to you.

49

Colin had an aunt on your grandfather's side called Phyllis – a disastrous bridge player, by the way: Colin would have taken money off her at cards if he could, but she never went to the clubs. She was a well-to-do woman, a spinster, and unlike your grandfather, she'd managed to hang on to her money. She lived modestly too, in a place off Campden Hill Road – but this is the thing, dear chap: Colin got the money out of Phyllis anyhow. Phyllis, you see, was an influential figure in the family. And she had an opinion of Colin. She thought he was no good – which is debatable – and she thought he was turning into a cad, which I think was true at the time. He needed to sort himself out, settle down, get a respectable living and so on. And once he'd run off with Maureen, Phyllis was keen that they should marry and have a child. She wanted him to put an end to his nonsense and grow up. We all did. "You'll have nothing from me until you make a better fist of things." That was Phyllis's message.'

Boris rubbed his eye and let his finger drop to the edge of his mouth.

'How do I know all this? Because when he and Maureen ran off together, they had nowhere to go, and Colin asked me could I put them up for a few days. I ended up sleeping on my own settee for three months, and we used to chat a lot in those days, your father and I.

'So, my dear chap, you were Colin's plan – something of a last resort. And a year or so later Colin said to me, in the greatest confidence, that Maureen had gone into hospital, she'd had a child and Phyllis had decided to help out financially with the new family. Mission accomplished.'

Somewhere the stirrings of a memory: a brief, intimidating image of Phyllis, huddled over a stick, her body like a bean-pod whose two ends are struggling against nature to become joined, and of a small boy, going forward to an armchair with fawn fabric, under orders to give her a kiss.

'Then I heard', Boris continued, 'that you were not Maureen's child, and it was all going to be hush-hush, a family secret – especially where Phyllis was concerned. I was one of the first people to know, and I kept the secret. Make what you will of it. You were their child, to all intents and purposes, and they looked after you. Phyllis started providing generous sums of cash, which Colin spent, and a few years later, she put up the money for his move away from Notting Hill, when they got their first place in London – all their own – somewhere off the King's Road – you probably remember better than I do. And Phyllis's death was no bad thing for Colin's finances either – that's as far as I know. Meanwhile, you were growing up and you were well looked after. And here you are, in reasonable shape. You're scarcely a confused kind of fellow, now, are you? And I'm sure Colin left you a few thousand pounds – I mean, he had no money, he went through so much of the stuff, and of course they were hard up in the end, but I don't suppose he cut you off. So I shouldn't worry about being a bastard, or any nonsense like that. Not if I were you . . .'

It was pure curiosity, I said, to want to know about my natural mother.

Evidently Boris, an intensely inquisitive man, thought curiosity was ill advised in this case.

'I'd leave it where it is,' he said. 'Perfect waste of time. And you can turn up things you'd rather not know.'

I said I imagined my natural mother was dead, and asked in passing if Boris had known one of Maureen's cleaning ladies, a woman called Mrs Privett. He looked disdainfully at me, as if I'd suggested a hand of cribbage.

'Did you know', he asked after a moment, 'that your father's bridge went badly downhill? He couldn't be bothered to keep up with the conventions.'

I felt unusually, pathetically eager to defend my father and perhaps inflict pain on Boris's poodle.

' . . . and the Lucan fellow,' I heard Boris say.

Colin had known Lord Lucan before the murder of his children's nanny in 1974 and his sudden disappearance. Drowned off Newhaven by one account; living under an alias in southern Africa by another. Colin had been intrigued by Lucan's disappearance, I remembered, and a touch demoralised: he'd been in the habit of separating Lucan from his petty cash three or four times a year at one or another club in London.

'Of course,' Boris said, 'the world is full of fairly good bridge players. There are endless Johnnie Lucans.'

We talked briefly about Colin's favourite club, the Portland. It was through his association with the Portland that Colin had taken part in a revision of the rules of contract bridge shortly before he died.

'Colin made a steady income at the club for quite a while,' Boris told me. 'I'd thought of joining when times were hard, but for one reason or another, it didn't happen.'

I lingered for a bit, dazzled by the ghosts of Christmases and New Years past. There had never been any cloud over Colin's propriety as a bridge player and certainly never any cheating scandals: he was spotless on that score. And for all Boris had to say, Colin was an attractive, unruffled figure, even when he played for stakes he couldn't afford to lose, and even when he lost. A man who felt the pressure of seductive indolence bearing down on him from his father's side of the family, and who reacted badly to the fey Edwardian charm of his mother.

Boris was a different matter. An aggressive, rowdy intellectual whose family had made its fortune in horses: thousands of sturdy pullers, purchased anywhere between the Baltic and the Crimea. They'd sold them in Britain, mostly to pit-owners in Yorkshire and South Wales, and then begun supplying the metropolitan omnibus companies in Paris and London. Boris had gone on to work in Hamburg and shuttled to Zagreb as a factor for the French army, buying whatever he thought looked good. He was a charismatic, dedicated bridge player, a dialectician who could argue any hand around. Above all, being Boris suited him, in a way that being Colin hadn't always suited my father.

'Tough little horses,' he said of his runs into Croatia, as he fussed the poodle.

It had just stopped raining when he and his wife showed me out.

'There are all kinds of bastards,' he said, backing into the hallway with a genial wave. 'Just remember you're one of the luckier ones.'

As the door closed, I thought I heard his wife take him to task.

I drifted up to Ladbroke Grove and turned into Chesterton Road. I walked to the junction with St Lawrence Terrace and took another look at number 22. What was I expecting? The sliver of a notion, something to go on.

I imagined Colin losing a shed-full of money at the Portland without letting on, a touch sour on the inside, until he won it back the following week. Or not. Never batting an eyelid, never letting on – this was one of the ways Colin used to hurt Maureen, again and again. But his imperturbability about money won or lost at cards was a kind of courage.

There was a trace of dusk about the early afternoon on Ladbroke Grove. As the cloud let up, a brief burst of sunlight raked a 52 bus. The inside of the lower deck glowed like a church, as though each passenger had lit a spill and held it up at the window.

Boris died a year or so after that meeting. In the interval, he'd won the world senior bridge pairs.

With my godfather to reckon in, the family landscape seemed strewn with casualties. Colin had been dead ten years. Then it had been my aunt Rosemary: she died not long after I'd visited Boris – this death was unexpected and shocking and I'd felt cheated by it, as one might feel in the face of a broken promise. Thereafter it got hard to keep track of the order. But I think Jill was next: she drank herself to death a year or so after her wild outing with Maureen in Notting Hill Gate. Finally, Maureen had managed to trade her own non-existence for a full-dress death. At the crematorium in Leatherhead, near her son Peter's house, the River Mole had burst its banks. The cloud had lifted after several days of heavy rain. It was a cold, bright autumn day. Floodwater sparkled on the lawns below the ceremonial building, built in the style of a supermarket, and there were shiny slicks either side of the cloister, where you half expected to find a cash machine in the wall. Looking across the water, I saw Maureen sitting in a boat, holding the cat, gliding over the hidden lawns towards one of the shacks and cottages she'd been obliged to live in with Colin. I remembered the ritual lighting of paraffin stoves to dry out the rooms; and then I wondered in a vague sort of way whether all this damp around the crematorium would make it hard to get a good blaze going under our mother.

Peter – son of Graham and Maureen, and by then a man in his early sixties – had transferred some old 8 mm footage on to a videotape, which he ran at the brief, jovial send-off after the funeral. There were glimpses of just about all the fallen, including Maureen and my aunt Rosemary and yes, I think maybe Boris as well, and poor Jill.

It was a touching occasion. In the old reels, Maureen looked charming and funny, with a range of hats and pretty dresses, period pieces in their own right, and in most scenes she was somewhere quite smart: a private club in Maidenhead, a golf tournament in another redoubt of the Home Counties, or a good full-scale wedding with a marquee. Under the various hats a ripple of fair hair, a flash of a smile, but the pale blue eyes always a bit elusive. And there she was at a family event, maybe a christening, with Colin and her first husband, the three of them chattering away – bring on the kidneys and scrambled eggs – then breaking off to stand motionless as people did in those days when they realised a movie camera was pointed their way.

Peter gave me a handful of oddments before I left, in a plastic bag with white and green stripes, folded over and taped down. There were some photos, he said, and some papers he thought I'd find interesting.

He used Maureen's old formula: 'The photos', he said, 'have what I call sentimental value.'

Driving away, I found myself singing one of Maureen's favourite songs, from *Oliver!* 'Consider yourself . . . well in, consider yourself . . . one of the family.' And I remembered a remark she'd made one of the last times I'd paid her a visit: 'It's no use you sitting here all day. Where do you live?'

Why look for the traces of another mother? I thought, as I drove back up the A3. One had been more than enough.

At home, I'd thought to inspect the photos in the bag, but there hadn't seemed much point bothering with the papers, and in a moment of lassitude – relief, I think it was – I decided not to open up the bag at all. I took it upstairs and lobbed it on to a pile of similar bags in a cupboard at the top of our house, where everything I meant to get around to one of these days had begun to expand, like the body of a large animal decomposing on a ledge in remote, temperate highland.

Maureen's death might well have been the signal to turn wholeheartedly to Margaret Walsh. But a year went by, then the better part of another, and instead I found myself preoccupied with Mother Two, and by extension Colin, and how little I'd known them. Yet there was no thinking about Maureen without the ghostly presence of Margaret hovering in the form of a question, and no turning to Margaret without the sense that she was being chaperoned this way and that by the things Maureen had said about her. I was astray in Indian country now – or Mother Country, as I'd come to think of it. I felt perplexed and stupid. It was scarcely a promising state of affairs. Nonetheless, to keep going over this ground might be to stumble on something useful; and in due course I did.

How and why had I come to think of Margaret as frail? It had largely to do with Maureen, I reasoned, and the story she told. The young girl – no, 'the little girl' – who appeared in the second or third telling hadn't really assumed the shape of an adult. She wasn't a mother in the sense that I understood it then or later. I gathered, or invented, the frailty of Margaret on the basis of Maureen's tellings. Even as she became an imaginative causeway into a bigger world, my notions about her were inflexible. First, she was in difficulty of some sort, constant and wearing, like waking up every morning to torrential rain or having to eat unappealing food; second, she was short; and third, like all the children I knew at the time, she wore sandals with a petal motif cut into the tops of the uppers. In other words, I saw her as a playmate a little older than I was, but nearer to me in age and disposition than Colin and Maureen, and perfectly ordinary: no sallowness in her cheeks, or rents in her clothes, that ordinariness unimpaired by her being in difficulty or – a linked circumstance – her being another of my mothers. For it also crossed my mind at about this time that I may have had several mothers.

No relation, either, between Mother Two and this would-be mother whom I might never encounter, except perhaps, as I came to realise later, vaguely, as an aspect of things: someone evoked when I was older by a poignant photograph of the post-war inner city, a pretty piece of crockery in a jumble sale or a discussion at school about illegitimate children.

Then my sense of her frailty took on another form. It was probably a few years later, in the 1960s, when the Victorian era was portrayed as a sulphurous hell in which every working-class child was driven up a chimney or down a pit and the world was run by a consortium of bullies with cold hearts and repressed appetites. And I have no doubt that when my gnarled great-aunt Phyllis dipped into her bank account for the dwindling sums that remained, now that so much was being lavished on Colin, and packed me off with Maureen to see *Oliver!* on the stage, I recognised a little of my absent mother in the character of Nancy. Margaret had suddenly grown up – and she'd become robust.

Nancy faded from my imagination, but Maureen never quite gave her up: the strong girl with the heart of gold on whom misfortune scowls, in the guise of a dissolute thug. She was one of Maureen's favourite stage characters – I'm not sure she'd read the novel – and *Oliver!* was one of her favourite shows. It was tender and harsh, and it was tender precisely because it was harsh – or was it the other way about? At the beating heart of the thing were a would-be mother in the form of Nancy and an orphaned child.

Only one heroine had mattered more to Maureen than Nancy. We'd been to see *My Fair Lady* during its first run in the West End, with the original London cast, before I was sent away to school. That would have been in 1958 or 1959. Maureen had promptly fallen in love with Eliza Doolittle. I remembered a lot about the show, and particularly Eliza's brassiness, her startling aversion to nonsense. But somehow in the transition to love and culture – a gruelling passage that leaves her exposed – I think I had an earlier glimpse of Margaret, an equivocal figure, moving around in the shadow of Eliza, part hardy working-class, part subtle and precarious, as the young Julie Andrews must have seemed in the part.

I couldn't have said any of it this way at the time, and the class fable – or is it a fable about essential human qualities? – was lost on me. But I grasped quite quickly how Colin and Maureen loved a cheeky cockney. And how they fell about when Stanley Holloway sang 'Get Me to the Church on Time'. Once they'd bought the soundtrack of the show, it became the theme music of our weekends, especially on Sunday mornings, an hour or so after breakfast, when Maureen would acquire her first target of the day, cruising the length of the living room – 'I could have spread my wings and done a thousand things' – banking suddenly in the direction of the drinks cabinet to obliterate a gin and tonic.

Maureen's infatuation with *My Fair Lady*, and my own fleeting association of Eliza with a mother I didn't know, had escaped me until now, and it didn't do to let things slip past, even if you weren't quite sure what purpose they served. I felt coolly self-satisfied. At the same time, it was as though three real people, Maureen, Margaret and myself, were converging fantastically on two characters drawn from the world of make-believe. It was the sort of convergence that takes place in dreams and it scared me somewhat.

Yet there was every reason to remain with Maureen. Quite apart from anything else, I ought by now to have had a clearer idea who she'd been. But her own past had been hidden. She never would say how she'd been orphaned or who the superb son, or daughter, of her superb grandmother actually was. Perhaps this concealment and the deception we'd set in motion about my own origins had something in common; and if so, might not Maureen's history be masked by the ampleness of her tale about her grandmother? As a small boy, I'd imagined this elderly lady – whom of course I'd never meet – to be a person of substance, framed by the big house with the driveway, and certainly as the key to Maureen's salvation. I only had to imagine the valises being packed for the mysterious journey to Egypt – I saw a stately ker-fuffle with plenty of staff – to grasp the grandeur of the arrange-ments and what they'd have meant to the orphan girl who later became my mother. But once I'd gone away to school, I began – a little priggishly, I think – to notice areas of murk and discoloration in the tapestry of Maureen's story, as though it had been ravaged by moths or vandalised with a bottle of bleach.

There was the fact, for example, that Maureen did not enjoy writing and kept her correspondence with me to a minimum. By the time I was twelve, I had it in my head that because she'd been brought up in a large house by a distinguished guardian, she should be a prolific letter-writer, or at least a regular letter-writer, like the mothers of my fellow boarders. At school the post was dis-tributed in a clumsy, offensive way. Ninety boys lined up along three walls of a large classroom while the headmaster stood with his back to the fourth, holding the mail. He would shout the name on each envelope or packet and flick it through the air or across the floor in the direction of the boy who'd answered 'Sir.' Haste and inaccuracy were the main features of this dispensation, with fortunate boys scrabbling under the desks for news from the out-side world – something Colin and Mim were able to supply more readily than Maureen – while others remained stoically pinned to the wall by their fading hopes.

And then in our various homes, life was remarkable for its absence of writing paper, pens and envelopes. To think of starting a letter was to know you'd have to turn the place upside down with little chance of success. The only concession to writing I remember was a dead ballpoint pen with a bit of chain at one end, which had once been attached to a stand advertising a golf club.

It was the same with books. For Maureen, there were only three. The first was a Bible with a hard, yellowish binding, ivory it was said; this was a baptismal gift to 'Jeremy' and signed by the com-poser Haydn Wood – a friend of Colin's parents, I suppose – who'd written the popular tune 'Roses of Picardy' in 1916. Above his signature, he'd copied out a few bars from the refrain, along with the words by Fred Weatherly. Maureen always kept a beady eye on the whereabouts of this bible, in case it was valuable and she had to head out on her own one day. Once – I'd have been nine or ten at the time – I was persuaded by Colin to help her unpack after a failed attempt to leave him. I found the bible among her belongings in a beige suitcase made by a company that Colin, by now a flourishing broker, was recommending to investors.

The other, far more important volumes for Maureen – the lapidary texts – were *One Hundred and One Dalmatians* by Dodie Smith and *The Incredible Journey* by Sheila Burnford. Her copy of *The Incredible Journey* was one of the few things that she managed to hang on to until the end of her days. It tells the story of two dogs and a cat who wander through Canada trying to get back to their owners, even though their owners are no longer where they were when the mystifying and painful separation occurred. In the course of the journey, the pets get into trouble with the less domesticated species. There is courage and sorrow, loyalty and heartbreak: all animal life is there.

Scattered about the house – we never quite got round to bookshelves – were a couple of titles by Ngaio Marsh, a batch of paperbacks by Dennis Wheatley and Ian Fleming and an incomplete, untouched set of Dickens in pale blue cloth bindings. Nobody went near the Dickens: Colin, a reader of contemporary paperbacks mostly, declared a hatred of him for his mawkishness about the poor and his long-windedness.

Maureen venerated the Dickens like a bequest – a dinner service that should have accompanied its owner to his death – which is how I realised the set was probably a gift from her first husband. She kept a respectful distance from it at all times. But she liked the Dodie Smith – maybe it was the source of the Dalmatians she remembered trotting behind as she sat in her grandmother's carriage. As for *The Incredible Journey*, she knew it well and could talk about the woes of its four-legged protagonists with the passion of an Arthurian scholar proposing a view of Camelot from the King's kennels. She stuck with these books, I guess, because she enjoyed stories about families getting separated – mine perhaps no less than hers – and was relieved to think such stories ended well. There is no question, either, about what her preference would have been if she'd had to choose between a world full of human beings and a world full of dogs. I don't know whether her managing to keep a grip of *The Incredible Journey*, long after she'd abandoned or mislaid almost every other possession, was evidence of the dog in her or the tenacious human being. It proved nothing about her habits as a reader: her boy was right in saying that Maureen had never been a book person. His mistake was to think that reading was proper to mothers in the way that offices were proper to fathers, or that children didn't really come out of a woman's body.

Then, when I was thirteen or so, Jill announced that our mother's horse-and-carriage story was rubbish. In those days, I hadn't given the information much thought.

Now, though, I wondered if it wasn't connected in some way to Maureen's romance with the idea of the poor working girl, which seemed to shed a glimmer of light on her character, or at any rate on her story, though I couldn't yet say what it clarified. There was the selfless, sturdy Nancy in *Oliver!* and there was, above all, the charmed, successful Eliza Doolittle in *My Fair Lady* (Maureen had certainly not read Shaw, for whom Colin evinced another of his hatreds). Nancy's songs were very much a feature of Maureen's repertoire, but with Eliza she had a daily complicity. Eliza's songs, both before and after Higgins's breakthrough, were forever on her lips. When she wasn't singing them out loud, you might catch her whispering them, as though rehearsing some sweet flattery. So, while all the songs seemed, in their different ways, to hint obscurely at my absent Mother One, they must have spoken to Maureen about someone far closer to home. And at some stage I must have wondered, as I was wondering now, whether that someone wasn't herself. I must also have harboured a suspicion that the marriages to Colin and his predecessor, the personable Graham, had brought Maureen a long way from her own origins. As the dissimulated adoptee, I might not have been the only member of our threesome who'd come up in the world.

You couldn't tell with Colin whether he was a covetous person given to ostentatious acts of generosity, or whether he had a core of generosity that was slowly overwhelmed, confining him to intermittent gestures of good will and prodigality. Either way, he was an excellent host and, very much to his credit in my eyes, a person who preferred to count the costs later rather than sooner. And so, in the middle of the 1960s, he indulged Maureen in a way that he never did again. Her dream was to become a flower girl herself, only posher than Eliza in the first instance: more, in fact, like the original Liza in the afterword to *Pygmalion*, who's left Professor Higgins's establishment, married Freddie Eynsford-Hill and opened a flower shop.

Maureen was already well prepared. She had begun working for a florist in South Kensington after I'd been away at school for four or five years and she'd gone on to run a stall near Rutland Mews. It was a success. Colin raised a loan and they rented premises off the Brompton Road.

Maureen's talent for arranging flowers was now obvious, dramatic even, and she was soon being patronised by London celebrities, whose names were a constant struggle for her. 'You know, darling, the actor!' she'd say of Michael Caine. 'The curly-haired one who kills all the nignogs with the hay tutus and enormous spears in that film your father likes. I call him Alfie.'

She sold arrangements to Jean Shrimpton, Alec Guinness, Tony Blackburn and others whose names she got confused. Names of flowers, too, were a struggle, even though she knew exactly what she had in mind: myosotis, chrysanthemum and anemone would come out sounding like rare distempers in farm animals. 'Pansies' was always said with an involuntary smile, even when she was referring to the flower itself. Or she might remark of a gay client: 'He's what I call a pansy.' And then: 'I love pansies, they have a wonderful sense of humour.'

There was a glamour about the cramped shop that made Maureen glamorous too, even when she worked herself into a state of exhaustion. As I thought of that time now, my teenage self seemed briefly – much too briefly, I felt – to be aligned with the little boy who'd prefigured him, both of them deeply fond of this person their mother. The brusque set of her face eased up, she wore less clogging foundation; the peekaboo eyes got bigger and took more in. Her hours were often very long, and in the four months or so that I'd be home from school, I found her mostly cheerful. She was good with the customers and good at the back of the shop, cutting and dressing, primping the fussier commissions, going by instinct to the simpler, more elegant arrangements, standing ankle-deep in stems or shuffling through green, powdery windfalls of floral foam.

There was normally a bottle of something near the kettle – gin or, around Christmas time, champagne, which the clients liked to give her. But upstairs, after hours, the mood was gloomy. Colin wasn't enjoying the new state of affairs: he complained of the mess; he'd rather Maureen was available to cook a meal at night after he got back from the club; he felt she had no head for business. All this he made perfectly clear. She soldiered on regardless.

She could no longer afford to have hangovers. Twice a week at five in the morning she'd have to be on the way to the market at Covent Garden to buy in stock. These trips were the high point of her week and when I was around I used to go with her. In the flower market, she seemed younger and funnier than I'd thought she could be, shy but oddly at home with the traders, confused about money, though sure of what she wanted to buy. For their part, they appeared to worship her. They fetched and carried for her with a mixture of deference and cheek – the caricature of the cockney working man that Colin and Maureen used to delight in – so that I saw her in quite another light from the narrow, unkind glare of family life. They called her 'Mrs H' or 'Maureen'. And she called them by their first names. She knew every one of them straight off, unlike the names of her celebrity customers.

The last time I recall driving back with her to Knightsbridge – at seven a.m. in sparse traffic, with an open box of white carnations on my lap and the tips of some loose gladioli prodding me in the ear – she was singing 'Wouldn't it be loverly?' It's the famous song that Eliza Doolittle sings while she darts about the barrows in Covent Garden at the beginning of *My Fair Lady*. A witty gloss on aspiration. But in which direction – up or down – was Mother Two hoping to go by then?

V

Ghosts

The work that Ann Pike had felt should be done, a thorough trawl through remembered things, seemed mostly concluded. But I was loath to stop and even if I'd wished to, I might have found it impossible.

I'd been living abroad for a year, and when I headed for London in the hope of establishing something real about Margaret Walsh, I was unable to travel light. I thought there were bits of the past I might jettison, but as soon as I tried to shear away a part, I became aware of the ductile quality of memory: it was as if I'd wanted to carve into warm pitch, or honey.

On the train up through France, I dozed and half-knew I was dreaming obliquely of Margaret. But when I woke to rolling woodland at the window, then a motorway, my vivid memory of the house in which the dream took place dispersed the details of the dream itself.

For years I'd refused to have any form of inner conversation about this place because I couldn't accept that it no longer existed. It was the most beautiful of Colin's mother's houses, very much more than a shack – a rambling pebbledash structure with two floors and a raised concrete walkway along the length of the front. She had called it Laughing Water, the name of Hiawatha's bride in the Longfellow poem.

Built midway between the houseboat and Rosemary Cottage, about twenty yards from the banks of the Loddon, Laughing Water was another of our early haunts where I'd spent my days as a little boy – summer weekends especially, under the alert eye of Colin's mother Mim, while he and Maureen took to the golf course. Mim presided generously over the house, the surrounding garden and the river bank, while small birds fluttered and toiled at her offerings of lamb fat on the strange clothes line stretched above the concrete walkway. In the evening she lured the ducks and moorhens off the river bank. She let me do as I pleased.

The rooms of the house were exquisite, upstairs and down. Their fine wooden panelling, quickened with a white polish, had begun to blister in places because of the damp. One entire side of the drawing room consisted of a leaded window overlooking a wide circle of rose bushes which flowered red and white through the summer. At the centre of the circle an old rambler blazed haphazardly over a decrepit metal arch. Between the big window and the fireplace, Mim had installed a white upright piano, which no one in the family could play and which I doubt had ever been in tune.

In the early days, there were gas lamps around the walls of the drawing room. A crude chandelier with four gas mantles hung from the ceiling over the circular dining table. The miraculous diffusion of light and the steady plainsong of the gas came, as I grew older, to stand in my memory for the idea of persistence. I might play around in my mind with a word like 'steadfastness', and the sound of Mim's gas lamps, the sight of the pale white panelling lit up with the intensity of a July morning, would tell me all I needed to know about the person I'd have liked to be. The gaslight became a comic image later still, when I remembered that the system ran on a shilling meter and there was a scrabble for the pile of coins on the sideboard as the light dimmed. Constancy at a price was the truer way to look at things.

The house was serviced by a well at the back. A grown-up would take a jug of water round to the cast-iron pump, prime it and set vigorously to work, leaving a tap open in the kitchen – also at the back – and listening out for the first gush to resound in the sink.

Under the far end of the building was a Stygian boathouse containing the waterlogged remains of two punts. Here Colin's parents had once taken shelter during the Second World War, in the belief that their remote part of England was about to experience the full fury of the Luftwaffe, as a lone British bomber limped overhead after a mission on the Continent. From the concrete roof of the boathouse you could mount an outside staircase on the end wall of the building and arrive at a low door beneath the gable. The door opened on to a neglected attic room, where I was discouraged from going. Above it, there was an inscription in metal lettering. It ran up the left side of the gable to the apex, then down the right, so that you had to tilt your head mid-course to read it – unlike the last page of a letter from Mim, the building itself could not be rearranged. It was a couple of lines from Longfellow: 'Beautiful is the sun, O Strangers, When you come so far to see us!'

When Mim died in 1972, I'd already had the use of the house for a few weeks in the summers – I was at university – and my feelings for it had grown. By then, of course, the gaslights had been replaced with electricity, which also powered the pump. One or two stopgap interventions had been made to hold off a collapse in the upstairs region. Laughing Water was otherwise quite unspoiled and ramshackle.

The things I associated with Mim were still in evidence: that circle of rose bushes, grown frayed and a trifle shapeless; two stands of bamboo, once rather military and now decidedly off duty, either side of the cracked walkway to the house; ragged poplars at the edge of the garden; and an enormous copper beech which, according to family myth, she'd persuaded to weep by suspending bricks from the branches in the days when Colin and Rosemary were children and called it the 'brick tree'.

When the train drew into Paris, all I remembered of my dream was an errand I'd had to run, somewhere at the back of the house. Later, in London, as I unpacked my bags and took up residence for the next few weeks with friends in the north of the city, I wondered whether the past I'd known but forgotten might now give way to a world of which I knew next to nothing. It was a foolish idea.

'I'm concerned with his time in Tobruk. You know, Tobruk –' said a gentle, elderly, flustered man with a plastic briefcase and spectacles propped back on his forehead.

'Tobruk?' said the assistant in the search room of the Family Records Centre.

'It was a military death. His name was Rivers, but they put him down as Rivières with an s, or Riviera, which is *French* for Rivers, d'you see, and I don't quite know how to go about this.'

I noticed, as I made for the registers, that he was wearing desert boots. There was little else to set us apart. People who consult the public record of births, marriages and deaths achieve a strange affinity with the material they're looking at, and in turn with each other. It's a curious phenomenon, impossible in a library, whose contents are too diverse. A register of births, marriages and deaths, on the other hand, is an endless compilation of details so alike in most aspects, and so regimented, that distinction disappears altogether. Poring over it with other citizens, I felt we were gradually shedding whatever it was that made us various, until we were merely numerous. Which is more or less how we appear in the register itself, stripped of our differences and set down, one with another, in long columns inscribed in the ledger.

It took a while to get the measure of the volumes themselves and to adjust to the ambitiousness of the project. It was impossible, I found, to run my eye down a page of entries without becoming acutely aware of the public nature of any life, and its points of contiguity with the state, at birth, at death and at the intervening stages of marriage or having children. Public record of this sort sent a shiver of dismay through Colin and Maureen, but I found something reassuring about it, and the modicum that men and women hold in common.

I'd decided on the green registers – marriages – as the best place to start. Often the mother who puts a child up for adoption will go on to get married, and she may do so fairly soon after the birth of her child. I settled on the third quarter of 1952 as a good starting point, and decided to call a halt at the end of 1956. I was putting Margaret Walsh somewhere between the ages of sixteen and twenty-two at the time of my birth.

From the outset, there were Margaret Walshes marrying thick and fast. They were marrying up north for the most part, in Rochdale, Wharfedale, St Helens, Newcastle, Durham North-East. There were a few marrying in the south: Eton, Hampstead and

was having supper with Colin and Maureen at one of Colin's shabby, expensive clubs in central London, when Maureen asked me, out of nowhere, if I'd felt awkward about being an adopted child. I was taken back by the question, and Colin, who preferred not to talk about our family's peculiarities, was visibly ruffled.

'Come on, darling, these are lunatic questions,' he said. 'Our son has come to see us. It's an occasion. I've brought you all to the club for dinner. Let him relax, for heaven's sake.'

'No,' I put in, half-heartedly. 'I'm glad I was adopted.'

'That's good, darling,' Maureen said, 'because I adore you really, you and the doggies of course, you are the only thing I ever, I mean in my entire life, really ever ever.'

Colin tapped the wine bottle and raised a knowing eyebrow.

'No,' Maureen protested. 'No, I won't have that, Colin. I'm not sloshed, not in the . . .' And then: 'That little Irish girl, you know, darling, what's-her-name, little Moira Welch, she had other children. After you, I mean. And she came to us . . . well, not her . . . but we were . . .' A short pause. '. . . approached, I call it, more than once, and I was asked if we wanted to adopt more babies, if you see what I mean. And those little babies, you see, they were your sisters. Your father thinks I'm tight.'

'My sisters.'

'Oh I wish I'd said something,' said Maureen with the whole Dalmatian Plantation fantasy creeping unmistakably over her, as she imagined a litter of amenable little puppies rolling at her feet.

I was charmed and aghast. Colin lit a cigar and blew the smoke past Maureen's ear.

'This is nonsense,' he said.

'Why didn't you adopt them?' I found the question impossible to stifle, even though it must have sounded sharp, or peevish.

Something was said about the cost of educating children, and then, on the subject of when these approaches were made, Maureen grew vague. Perhaps when I was four or five years old – or was it earlier? Colin said nothing, and as quickly as it had blown up, like a squall over the half-eaten cutlets, the matter was dropped.

Leaving the club, I helped Maureen into her coat and brushed the dandruff from the shoulders of Colin's suit before she could make a vengeful, attentive fuss about it and perhaps fall over in the process. I was always struck, when I performed these rituals of departure, how small both Colin and Maureen were. It must have got harder, as the years went by, to keep the origins of their little boy secret. How does a pair of miniature horses pretend to the rest of the ménage that the gangly specimen in their corner is the straightforward outcome of a good day's rutting?

Maybe my sisters were tall as well.

To turn from the green registers to the red, from marriages to births, guided by what Maureen had said years ago, was to envisage a short-cut, and of course to envisage a sibling rather than a mother – a sister in her forties, say, quite likely still alive.

More than a short-cut, then: an excursion in its own right.

The green marriage indexes stood in the centre of the search room, generously apparent, but the red indexes, for blood and birth, were situated to one side, pleasantly confined, like the maternity wing of a hospital. I began in the first quarter of 1953.

In the birth indexes, the maiden name of the mother is given, but not her first name. I proposed to note down all the children born as Walshes to mothers with the maiden name of Walsh, on the assumption that they were probably 'illegitimate' – this was the terminology of the day – and that my own Mother One, if she'd gone on as a single parent to have more children, could well be in this index. I wouldn't know until I had a child's birth certificate in my hands, because only then would I ascertain the mother's first name. If I did find a Margaret Walsh who'd had children by the name of Walsh a few years after I was born, those children would be worth trying to follow up, even though there was no guarantee that their Margaret Walsh was my Margaret Walsh.

The first red volume yielded up three girls born Walshes to Walsh mothers, all of them in London and one of these in Kensington, a short way from Hammersmith. Anne, Elizabeth and Janet: the names were unremarkable, but in the splendid impartiality of the indexes, both monolithic and minimalist – names, dates, places, reference numbers, the same formula repeated several million times – they stood out like little illustrations in a primer. I felt drawn to the name Janet: I could almost see a Janet standing at the station exit where we'd agree to meet, probably by phone, after the introductory letter.

In the next quarter there were five Walsh children from Walsh mothers, only two of them girls, both born in the East End. Hardly my Margaret's domain, yet there was no knowing where she might have got to, and so they were likely suspects.

I was puzzled by the boys; inconvenienced even. What to make of Christopher, Leonard, Frederick and Geoffrey? What if Maureen had been half right? Right, I mean, about Margaret Walsh having other children, but wrong about their being girls? I tried to imagine a brother – a Leonard, say – with whom I'd sit once or twice a year in a pub within walking distance of the cemetery where our mother was buried, talking carefully, perhaps intently, about who she'd been and what had become of us. He might have traced her. He might even have met her before she died. He'd have a studio portrait. He might have something that belonged to her – a square of lace, a pile of 45 rpms or a ring. We'd exchange news and photos of our own children, speak about family likeness and then we'd have one for the road.

Even so, I'd lived with the dim possibility of sisters for thirty years and I wasn't going to throw everything up in the air for Leonard.

In the third quarter of 1953 there were no Walsh-to-Walsh girls at all. I began to feel out of sorts.

On leaving the building, I walked south along Rosebery Avenue and headed west. I got on to Guilford Street and rounded Coram's Fields – Thomas Coram, the former seaman, built his foundling hospital here in the 1740s – and cut through Queen Square in the direction of Holborn. I could see Maureen moving across the rough grass at the side of Rosemary Cottage in summer, with bread for the goose. Nothing about stray sisters at that stage.

What, I wondered, was the source of the harshness and dispatch in all my dealings with Maureen once I'd reached the age of eight or nine? Or earlier perhaps. Now she was in the kitchen of the cottage. Her little boy was about to taunt her. 'You're a witch!' He bolts around the sofa, the rug surfs over the old floorboards and then he's racing out across the wooden deck, laughing. He's down the steps and on to the grass, running towards the river and turning on the flat of his left foot, to angle off at the water, moving along the bank. I could still feel the turn he made and still know how it was to have a mother to oneself, a river of one's own, a gift for provocation followed by swift evasive action.

In those days, though, there was a bond between us. We had determined roles (a mother and her son) that held us fast. The bond had simply failed to evolve into friendship. Wasn't that it? But 'bond' and 'role' were words I never really got the hang of – they came, I thought, from one of the many voices, neither cherished nor particular, that kept me company in the world. So I couldn't be sure what 'failed' meant either, except that in my own eyes I stood accused of something.

I suppose I'd wanted to train the superb images of early childhood – of Maureen and Colin at that time – up the trellis of a much later period, when she was strong and funny and admirable, at the time of the flower shop, and to fashion her memorial. It didn't appear to be working.

On the subject of a 'bond', I reasoned – in Maureen's defence rather than mine – that she had surprised and amused me as we'd both grown older, but that I was too irritated or put off by the things she said to become her friend. That was in part because I could be obtuse. I could not, or would not, make sense of the way she spoke about us, about Margaret, about the existence of sisters. All that was better left as a series of unanswered questions at the back of our lives. Was she a fabulist, or simply a truthful person whose way of insisting on the facts had been to adorn them past the point of being credible? Or might she simply have been taking long-term evasive action of her own?

I'd got as far as 1954 in my search for Walsh sisters. Already it felt like a route march. It was tempting to think of the registers as a venture in social mapmaking, but this was to envisage the society they recorded as a polar landscape, flat and snow-covered: a world of white fabric – maternity linen, bridal outfits and winding cloth. Besides, in the registers, all the contours of the British class system were flattened, achieving a deceptive parity. A register of births, marriages and deaths was less like a map than a long shingle spit. You moved across it in your own time, as best you could, prospecting for whatever it was you had in mind. Your discoveries would be a matter of indifference to other prospectors, and their own to you. What we had in common was a lonely business, after all.

In the great spaces of the register I was prey to mirages: certainties based on nothing more than the sound of a first name; flurries of doubt and double-checking occasioned by the smallest piece of evidence – the discovery of Walshes with an 'e', for example. As myriad lost kin seemed to rise and subside again before my eyes, I realised that the search room was a place of obsession and that I'd lost no time succumbing to it.

By the time I was back with the registers, I'd grown a little easier with the idea of brothers. And with the siblings of 1954 I was spoiled for choice: in addition to three Susans, a Theresa, an Angela, a Sally, a Lavinia and a Marian, there were four Michaels, a John, a Gerald and a Patrick. The maiden name of the mother was a matter of doubt in one case only – maybe a Walsh or maybe a Walshe.

The announcement that the search room would shortly be closing coincided with the last quarter of 1956 and a nearly final count of sixty-two possible brothers and sisters, born out of wedlock to the closed ranks of Walsh mothers, all of them marching in step, it seemed to me, towards a night on the town in the early 1950s, and going on from there, as solid as a Roman tortoise formation, to overrun the maternity units of London and the south-east.

I took a hurried look at 1957. Skimming rapidly but surely along the first quarter, I found a Walsh baby by the name of Carol, born in Willesden, and another with no name – the index stated simply 'Girl' – born in Hammersmith. Among the many thousands of typed columns I studied, Carol's birth was one of the few entered in longhand. Carol was a plausible sister, and so was the Girl. Girl very much so, I thought. It was too late to fill out an application for the birth certificates. I noted down the references, levered the last volume on to its shelf and left the Family Records Centre in better spirits.

I woke up in the night, troubled and exhilarated by the beckoning wastes of the search room and the immensity of the information lying there. The following morning I walked south from Camden Town, picked up a 38 bus on New Oxford Street and entered the search room a few minutes after the Centre opened. I filled out application forms for four birth certificates: Carol from Willesden and the nameless girl delivered in Hammersmith in 1957, as well as two other children born between 1953 and 1956 that I'd noted. For this to go anywhere, the full name of the mother in column five of one of the certificates would have to be Margaret Walsh. Then I handed them in, along with the forms that would provide me with the marriage certificates over which I'd hesitated earlier.

Ladbroke Grove, Hammersmith Hospital, the White City Estate. Those neighbourhoods of west London, with their high numbers of immigrant Irish, had contained many Walshes in the 1950s. But was that a reason to assume that Margaret or any of her children might still be there? If she'd been poor for most of her life, then she may well have been on the move, at the mercy of events, available jobs, perhaps even men. If, on the other hand, she'd done well, she might have rediscovered her connections with Ireland, or retired miles from her old haunts. Even so, everything now seemed to be pointing west and the trick, I supposed, was to keep to a westerly course. Sooner or later some vestige of Margaret Walsh would turn up. Where the sun sets, the inquiry would end. The west was supposed to be a place of endings. I imagined the long shadows pitched out on Ladbroke Grove at dusk.

But my fixed bearing also led back inexorably to Colin and Maureen and the flat below Colin's parents. And I remembered the name of the street: Airlie Gardens. There was no returning to

75

this beautiful, memory-thickened part of the city without some sense of beginnings and middles, as well as ends.

Songs always seemed to end things, or mark off intervals, in Colin and Maureen's life. The end of the morning proper, and the prospect of late morning drinks, would involve Maureen singing gaily for half a minute; at weekends, lunch would only be concluded when Colin wandered over to browse the disorderly record collection; bedtime would be foretold by the last jingle on TV for a toothpaste or a remedy for indigestion.

On the Central Line, heading towards Notting Hill Gate, I realised that the extent of my adoptive parents' pasture, and its patchy nature, meant it was always in need of some unifying element. Journeys by car helped to consolidate the mental geography, from west London to the backwaters of the Thames, but music, too, did its share of the work.

By the 1960s, with reliable electricity in their places by the river, Colin and Maureen could play our theme tunes wherever they wished. Colin's repertoire of songs was drawn from the last throwbacks to music hall: Flanagan and Allen, for example. Here and there his tastes coincided with Maureen's. Sinatra always helped them to see eye to eye on a Saturday evening by the river when marital devotion was getting threadbare. They loved Ella Fitzgerald and Bing Crosby and Nat King Cole. These competent, virtuoso styles filled the summer weekends with an adhesive melancholy, but they were the theme music of my parents' managing to rub along tolerably for a few hours – Maureen discreetly at the cooking sherry in the kitchen, Colin smoking in the garden, as the unbearable strains of 'When I Fall in Love' wafted from the gramophone to die somewhere by the asparagus beds at the side of the septic tank.

There were the songs from *West Side Story* and the movie *High Society* – songs familiar to me because Colin and Maureen had the 33 rpm recordings. There were also the songs that Maureen took to as she twisted and hummed her way through the 1960s, leaving Colin in the dust, with her love of Frank Ifield ('What could be worse', Colin asked, 'than a yodelling Australian?'). But the songs we shared, the songs I hadn't forgotten or shaken off, any more than the hymns I sang at school, were the old ones from *My Fair Lady* and *Oliver!* As the train rattled cheerfully along between Bond Street and Marble Arch, I found I could recite the treacly verses of 'Where is Love?' from *Oliver!* Found, too, that I could hear Maureen saying, 'Oh dear, that poor Oliver always breaks my heart. Who was that little actor again?'

I don't know that it ever crossed my mind to imagine a likeness with young Oliver. In the novel, I grasped soon enough, his adoption was a conjuring trick that reunites him with his dead mother's family. As bosoms go, Mr Brownlow's was hardly ample, but he was related to Oliver by marriage, while Rose Maylie, who comes under Brownlow's wing when they all go off to live in the country, has turned out to be Oliver's aunt. Blood retrieved blood, then, as progeny clambered up through the mire of nineteenth-century London to discover its source. This was not so much an adoption, the way I understood it, as a coincidence masking the workings of an uncanny homing instinct.

Mostly the story of Oliver Twist put me in mind of a far-off girl – a young woman by then – somewhere in the city.

At Notting Hill Gate, I made my way up Pembridge Road. I had some absurd fantasy that I'd still find the Galleon, an old haunt which served braised pork chops and peas in the 1970s. It was long gone. I sat in a Starbucks, failing to recreate a cup of Galleon tea from the pale Darjeeling served in a latte mug, and thinking that maybe the music in our family wasn't just the reassuring sound of continuity between one of our redoubts and another, but a way of hearing the world at large.

Back in the days when I used to eat at the Galleon, I'd discovered a hidden coupling between *Oliver!* and *My Fair Lady* that allowed the two to be hooked up and shunted to and fro at the back of my mind as a single train. I'd been watching the Carol Reed film and noticed that Shani Wallis, the actress who'd played Nancy, did a passable cockney in dialogue, but the most important numbers were sung in something resembling Queen's English.

In a plot involving poor Londoners, cockney was as indispensable as ragged shirts, bare feet, big tits and gin vats, but songs in a musical sidle away from the demands of the story to open up a different sort of space for the characters. In *Oliver!*, these transcendent interludes could clatter off into cockney, provided they were fun. But Nancy's were done in posh, partly because speaking posh hadn't yet become contemptible, and partly because if you talked cockney, you talked without the authority that the musical hiatus required. Above all, I figured, watching the film, Nancy is a proper young woman, and a proper young woman has soul, and to make that point she had to be given respectable vowel sounds.

It was this question of the soul that seemed to make Lionel Bart, or Carol Reed, a descendant of George Bernard Shaw – the Shaw of *Pygmalion*. 'You have no idea', Henry Higgins says to his mother about Liza (as she is in the play), 'how frightfully interesting it is to take a human being and change her into a quite different human being by creating a new speech for her. It's filling up the deepest gulf that separates class from class and soul from soul.' A modern Higgins might want to take a 'lady' and teach her Estuary English – the experiment is in theory the same – but when all souls finally communed in Shaw's model society, they were unlikely to do so in cockney.

Not long after I'd assembled this little train, I began toying around and discovered another way to conjugate its parts. In two of the big singalong pieces from *Oliver!* led by Nancy, she is allowed a bit of cockney latitude. 'Oom-Pah-Pah', of course, but also 'It's a Fine Life', another convivial tavern piece, with Bill Sikes on the scene but not yet fully menacing. 'If you don't mind avintergo without things, it's a fine life,' Nancy chirrups lustily, and the chorus echoes, 'Fine life'. Or near enough. And so it was that when I first read *Pygmalion*, I was astonished to hear a foretelling of the song in one of Higgins's outbursts to Liza, at the end of the play, when she deserves a show of kindness from him. 'If you can't stand the coldness of my sort of life, go back to the gutter . . . Oh, it's a fine life, the life of the gutter. It's real: it's warm: it's violent: you can feel it through the thickest skin: you can taste it and smell it without any training or work.'

With the new arrangement I'd happened on in my marshalling yards came the quaint dilemma of how to describe a world I knew very little about: the one way, from *Oliver!*, cast its inhabitants as a vital, stoical lot with their wits about them, while the other saw the 'fine life' for the coarse, uninflected thing it was, when viewed with due deliberation by the luckier kind of bastard.

It was this ugly dilemma that had produced so many contortions during the 1970s, as young people who'd come through expensive British private schools and then universities, and whose sympathies lay to the left, began trying to erase their class origins by contriving a downswing in their accents. It was, indeed, a little like the Higgins experiment in reverse. In my late teens and early twenties, I was very much part of this and by the time I started eating at the Galleon, I bore an improbable resemblance – I see this now – to my grandmother's gardener. I preferred the kinds of shirt I'd worn for a while at boarding school, but without the detachable collars, and old pinstripe waistcoats from jumble sales. In those days I was working on a playground in Hammersmith. Quite a lot of graduate staff cultivated the same image. How odd it must have seemed to the parents in the nearby housing estate to confide their children to a bunch of young borough employees who thought like clergymen but spoke like expensive football transfers and dressed like something out of *Mary Poppins*.

Maureen had been appalled.

'It's embarrassing, the way you look,' she'd remarked. 'Even my doggies are scared of you, aren't we, Suki? Is it because you're adopted? In my entire life I've never seen such a chip on anyone's shoulders, not even Pinocchio, and if it gets any longer I can't think *what* will become of you.' Then the sadness in the eyes which signalled an end to hostilities, and the memory of taking me to see *Pinocchio* at the Essoldo on the King's Road. Possibly. '*You* remember, with Jill. You were such an adorable little boy then and you loved what I call a Walt Disney.'

I thought now that I might have worn anything, said anything, even delivered my mother's dogs into the hands of the Baader-Meinhof Gang: she'd have been happy with a modest show of affection from Colin and me. Neither he nor I went in for that kind of thing.

Like Liza rebuking Higgins, Maureen used to say of Colin that he was too reserved. She would brace herself for the five-syllable word that lay, what, a sip of gin and tonic from the end of the sentence she had in view, and she'd approach it with caution: 'Your father is very under the, you know, darling, Colin is a . . . he's just a very. I don't mind too much. You know he's always been that sort of a. Sort of a man I suppose you'd call it, actually. He's not what I think of as . . .' And then, turning away from me to address him directly: 'You're what I'd call, it's not just *me* saying this, everybody we know says you're, well, you're what I call undemonstrative.'

Two of everything. Two musicals, two mothers. Two carriages stranded in a siding. And a pair of undemonstrative men.

VI

Bearings

Electoral rolls feel good in the hand and good for the mind. They
have nothing to do with genealogy, though the most bloodthirsty
researcher may forsake the indexes of births, marriages and
deaths for local voting records, in order to track down a distant
cousin.

Chesterton Road was the logical place to begin another hunt for
Margaret Walsh, and Kensington Public Library housed a set of
electoral registers for the Ladbroke Grove area. She'd cited number 22 in 1952 and I set off three years earlier, at 1949, in the ward
of St Charles, when the building had already been converted into
flats and contained half a dozen eligible voters. I continued up to
1952, but there was no sign of a Walsh. I went through to 1956.
Still nothing. That would mean she'd been too young to vote in
1952, but at the least I'd hoped for an older brother, an uncle, who
knows, maybe a father and mother in the records. I doubled
back again, looking for Irish names, and scanning the residents
of number 24 at the same time. There was a Mary Carroll and later
a Clare O'Brien. When someone moved or died, I made a note of
the date they last appeared in the roll, but the signs so far were not
encouraging.

I began browsing: free-ranging either side of Chesterton Road
to nearby streets, in search of Walshes. There were two on Kensal
Road who fell off the rolls in the late 1950s, but neither was a
Margaret.

Then there was Rillington Place, a few pages away in the same
ward. In 1945, the entry for number 10 included 'Christie, Ethel'
and 'Christie, John Reginald'. In 1949 they were joined by the ill-
fated 'Evans, Timothy J.'. Evans's name did not appear in 1950.
He'd been put on trial in January for the murder of his daughter –
the Crown had thought a conviction more likely for Geraldine

than Beryl – and hanged in March. Christie and his wife remained on the roll. They were joined in 1952 by 'Brown, Beresford'. Brown was a Jamaican immigrant who'd moved into the top flat so dramatically vacated by the Evans family. There'd been no sign of Mrs Christie since before Christmas, and in the spring of 1953, with Christie absent, too, the landlord agreed to let Brown use the kitchen in the ground-floor flat. When he began putting up a shelf for his radio, he uncovered three bodies.

The electoral roll for 1954 shows a clean sweep at number 10. No Browns, no Evanses or Christies. The house had become a respectable establishment, but still deeply sinister, occupied only by a George and Patricia Lawrence and an Esther Hart.

I don't suppose Christie meant more to me than he did to any other Londoner. But he'd achieved infamy, which is a way of remaining real, and his name in the register was as palpable as his deeds. I fell into a kind of despair about Margaret. I was beginning to think that only disreputable people left a mark in the world.

I took a break and walked along Kensington High Street, past the church of St Mary Abbots, where Maureen used to say I'd been christened. I might have checked – in Maureen's generous way of seeing things, a nice church was only a thought away from a carriage jingling through the gateway to a nice house – but there was no point.

Kensington High Street was a good place just now. In its grabby, know-nothing way, it reassured me that there was no harm in looking for a lost person. Or getting your nose out of the books for twenty minutes. Suddenly the 'search', as adoption people call it, was going swimmingly, even if four hours in the library had been fruitless.

It was a bookish sort of cheer, to do with the shift I'd made from the blood-and-marriage registers to the electoral rolls. I liked poring over the sociology of the city on paper, relying on numbered houses and polling districts and a sense of the geography. And of course it was a welcome change from the Family Records Centre to feel the density of all those adult lives disposed in ways that cut across the logic of kin.

It was late November. The shop windows were sprayed with glitter – mostly on the south side of the road, where Maureen used to tow her child so patiently around the old stores years ago: Barkers, Pontings, Derry & Toms.

Would she have worn a hat? I wasn't sure, but she used to complain of sore feet, and often, if we stopped for a cup of tea in one of the store cafeterias, she'd slip off her shoes. And wasn't that her little boy, peering under the table to examine the maternal feet, vaguely apparent in the nylon, with a seam crossing the top of the big toe, suggesting the figure of a man behind a net curtain? After a refill of tea, the shoes were slipped on discreetly, the bill was paid, Mother Two was revived and her small charge was beside her on the High Street, kitted up for his London life and Christmas coming on.

'Good care,' I remembered as he passed St Mary Abbots on the way to the bus stop on Kensington Church Street. 'Baptised.'

In the photo of the christening, Maureen has a hair-band studded with pearls. She has made herself up to look like a stage rodent: I'm thinking of the rats that once terrified me in a pantomime Dick Whittington. The baby is sullen and inscrutable: pointless to wonder where it thought it was. It is wrapped in a long shawl and at first sight preparing to levitate, though on closer inspection the opposite seems true: it has plummeted through thin air and Maureen, having broken its fall at the last moment, now has it in her arms as though it had been there all along. Colin, who is wearing a bowler hat and earning £1,200 a year on the London Stock Exchange, looks very much as if he'd just got away with an ingenious robbery. His generous aunt Phyllis would have been at the church. So would Boris, his friend and detractor. Almost everyone present would have known what this occasion meant for Colin, whose future had begun, all of a sudden, to look rather bright.

The bound volumes were where I'd left them on the desk at the back of the library. I was nagged by a neighbouring house, number 20 Chesterton Road, and thought I'd failed to note down the occupants' names. I was wrong about that. I lifted my head from the rolls and gazed down the length of the library.

When I went back to the 1952 roll, my eye strayed one column to the right of the Chesterton Road entries and lighted on a section of Ladbroke Grove. I couldn't believe I'd missed it earlier. I stood up, took a brisk turn around the desk, sat down again and read the names over.

'Privett, Lilian' and 'Privett, Peter' were registered as occupants of 141 Ladbroke Grove.

Surely this was the one. I started tracking Maureen's ex-char lady and her husband forwards from 1952, knowing it was only a matter of time before they dropped out of the running. Already, I was afraid to part with them. The trick was to go slowly, but it didn't work and sure enough, quite shortly they were gone. I jumped forward to the 1980s – maybe a son would be back – but it was a crazy thought that the Privetts would re-emerge in the same place.

Two shelves away stood a collection of old London phone directories. In 1985, there was a subscriber by the name of Peter Privett living out in Arnos Grove, to the north, and another living in east London, but no Lilian. The east Londoner disappeared from the 1992 directory, but Peter Privett of Arnos Grove was still there. The library's editions of the phone directory stopped in 2000: it would be a piece of great good fortune to find a Peter Privett intact so recently. I opened the volume gingerly, like a poacher who means not to startle an animal, located the pages and, without drawing breath, cast my eye very gingerly a little way beyond the Prices and Prides. I set the directory down on the nearest desk, made a note of the number, along with the address, and left the library.

The voice on the other end of the line was congenial. Elderly and sunny. I began by apologising – 'out of the blue,' I said – but I'd been going back over a bit of family history and the name Privett had come up: Privetts of Ladbroke Grove, back in the 1950s this would have been. A Mrs Privett, above all.

'That's my wife Lilian,' Peter Privett said. 'We were in Ladbroke Grove all right. We had a shop there for a few years after the war, but I'm afraid I can't help you. Lilian passed away eighteen years ago.'

I'm not sure what I'd have felt about someone calling me cold in the way I was calling Peter Privett. I'd have been suspicious and curious, but the man I was speaking to was relaxed. I imagined him on his feet, stooped somewhat to look out of the living-room window. And the definitive view from almost any London house: a prospect of cars in motion, or more probably parked. The thing was, I'd reason to think that Lilian Privett knew my parents, or had something to do with another person in our past called Margaret Walsh, a young girl in those days.

There was a long pause.

No, he didn't recall the name.

Maybe she worked in the shop? I asked. I was thinking of 'Counter Assistant, Chain Stores', the entry under column five of the original birth certificate, even though the Mackenzie Close address was a way from Ladbroke Grove.

And if she did work in a shop, perhaps it was a Chain Stores?

A shorter pause.

'Well, it was a chain of stores, if that's what you mean. They weren't called stores in those days.' Then, with a resigned laugh: 'No, Lilian would have remembered any girls. She had a good memory for names.'

I told him my family name.

No, sorry, he didn't recall it.

'This Margaret Walsh,' I said, 'I wonder if Lilian would have known her. The difficulty Margaret had . . . the difficulty was, she had a child she couldn't hang on to – and Lilian helped to have the child adopted. And I think that this Margaret Walsh . . . I've a feeling she was my mother.'

'That would have been typical of my wife,' said the voice after a moment. 'She looked after people, you see, and she had plenty of friends and acquaintances, a lot more than I did. A young girl gets pregnant . . . Lilian would have sorted something out for her. Yes, that sounds like my wife.'

I asked Peter Privett if I could pay him a visit.

85

That would be fine, he said.

'I could manage tomorrow,' I said, 'if you're free.'

He wasn't, and we agreed on the day after. He told me how to get to the flat.

'Come at dinner time,' he said, 'and I'll make you a toasted sandwich.'

The way it seemed to me, Maureen had never met Margaret Walsh, though it was just possible Colin had. He never said he had or hadn't. But because the arrangement wasn't made through an adoption agency, Colin handled all the preliminaries – trying to firm matters up, for instance, through the mediation of the cleaning lady, whose name I now knew was Lilian, and perhaps, too, advancing some money, again through Lilian, to frail young Margaret as she entered the last phase of the pregnancy.

'We made sure she was all right,' Maureen had said once, assuming her loftier manner with a sweetness that threatened to turn it into the purest affectation. 'And that's because we were sure she was a lovely girl and she needed our help.'

I'd approached this new information with caution. Even when they were arm in arm, Maureen and her notion of the facts were a little unsteady on their feet.

'You see, darling,' she went on, 'the poor thing was only little – and working in Woolworth's. Oh dear. And we tried to get a bit of money to her. We did, now I think of it. Your father did.'

It would have been unlike me to ask how much. I'd have wondered about my name, as I usually did, and whether it had been ordered up in advance, in the event of a boy. (What would they have ordered for a girl?)

Once they'd got the child, there'd have been the business of legalising the procedure, notifying the local authority – the London County Council – and the courts, and satisfying both that everything was as it should be.

Which still left a few technicalities. Not with regard to the law: in this, everything appeared to be above board. But how was the fact of the adoption kept from Colin's parents at this critical stage?

86

Colin had said, I think, that Maureen had been booked into a nursing home, where our little trio had convened for the first time before proceeding home, to celebrate the birth of a healthy little Harding with his parents and Rosemary. Is that actually what Colin said, or merely what I have in mind when I try to remember it? Hard to tell.

It was unlikely that Maureen would have been in a nursing home if there was nothing the matter with her, nothing remotely pregnant there at all. But Colin would have been at the hospital, surely? If only to pick up the baby.

Not necessarily. Someone else might have ferried it to a neutral point – and if Lilian Privett had befriended Margaret Walsh, she might have been the one to do so. Ever since I'd heard of Mrs Privett, I'd had a notion she might have played a part in this occult phase of the story called 'getting the baby'. But it was obvious from her husband's remarks on the phone that we'd never know.

There were thirty shopping days or so to Christmas, and a day to kill before I could meet Peter Privett – in Arnos Grove, a little too far east for me to think much would come of it. A canopy of low pressure had invested Camden – the whole of London – and spread across it like a punishment. I lay in bed, feeling the irresistible lure of the Family Records Centre. Not a useful thing to do: the certificates I'd ordered wouldn't be ready yet. Even so, it seemed a safe place, and a good wet-weather plan. I could work my way through more Walshes and who knows, maybe a Privett or two. When I shut my eyes and rolled over, I saw the shelves full of bound indexes turning into scored flanks of rock. I saw the doors opening at nine a.m. like a screen drawn back from the mouth of a cave, and heard a terrible rustling as thousands of bats teemed into the room and fastened everywhere in clusters.

Acting on a whim, I got off the Central Line train at Shepherds Bush, not White City. I walked up the Uxbridge Road and bought a handful of fresh green chillies from a Lebanese store. A little *madrasa*, hunkered in a recess, took me by surprise. I hadn't been here for a year or more.

I turned north along Bloemfontein Road towards the dark, coppery edge of the White City Estate. The plan was to walk, and to think my way to a sort of dawdling, undistracted state of vacancy and wait for something to fill it. Faint drizzle had cut the colour of the brick to muddy bronze. I wiped my spectacles on my scarf and pressed on into the estate, bearing right into Australia Road.

The clear-headedness I'd hoped for was clouded by a sense that this was indeed a walk through a graveyard: not the place where my Margaret died, but another place like Chesterton Road where her *trail* was likely to go dead. Yet padding through the estate, as I'd done before, was a sort of antidote, a walking cure, for certain habits of mind I'd acquired from Colin and Maureen, not wholly dislodged.

Colin would have said what he said about anything to do with privilege and modesty of means: that public housing was for an inferior breed of creature and it was organised at the expense of people like himself. (The handsome head is tilted up, the diminutive body a touch crumpled, the cigarette – a Players Navy Cut – is held low in the fingers, near the knuckles; a faintly insolent smile crosses the lips.) Maureen, for all she felt about feisty working people, would have concurred. I mightn't have shared these views, but there was a Colin-and-Maureen-like anxiety in me about the word 'public', about where you fit in and where you don't. The White City Estate and every push for public housing from the late nineteenth century on – this heroic attempt to bring order to the chaos of slum dwellings – was a challenge to our magical insularity. It spoke of a 'them' and an 'us', and we were squarely, tautologically, on the side of us.

I continued deeper into the quiet, almost trafficless space of the estate.

For Colin, and to a lesser extent for Maureen, Them and Us was a simple matter of being accountable to no one. Disdain was Colin's forte.

On Commonwealth Avenue, two women clambered from a red Vauxhall saloon and ran down the path to a block on my right while the driver, a man, sat with the engine ticking over.

Colin would have said. Colin would have said. What words are you about to put into that ironic mouth? That you'd only ever find two kinds of people who took an interest in public housing projects if they didn't live on them: vicars and sociologists. Three if you included communists, but in Colin's book, all sociologists and many vicars were communists in any case. Look at Canon Collins, a man of the cloth who gave succour to the Soviet Union every Easter as he passed within five miles of our watery enclave on the Ban the Bomb march to the nuclear weapons design centre at Aldermaston.

Yet there were more reasonable ways of figuring out where you stood in the bigger picture, as part of the thing we used to call society. Colin got it wrong and maybe I was in the lifelong process of getting it wrong in my own way. At the top end of Australia Road I set off back towards Bloemfontein Road, beginning to think how much we had in common, Colin and the boy from nowhere, father and son for a moment there. After all, this place he'd have loathed – this triumph of civic reasonableness – sent me into flurries of obscure anxiety.

The frayed outer edge of the din from the Westway was audible now as a vague but continuous groan. Six lanes, of which the three outward bound were nearest the estate. Cars and trucks were seething west. Within an hour, some of them would be out beyond the most westerly point of my childhood turf. But this was the way we never came. We could have headed for Holland Park Avenue and on to the A40, but we were Great West Road people, A4 people.

The soporific smell of our old Humber, then another car, yes, a Wolseley – equally overpowering. In due course, a Triumph Herald followed by a Triumph Vitesse with a radio, coinciding roughly with the opening of the M4, which thrilled Colin and Maureen as motorways thrill us all at first. Fewer grey, headachy smells in the later cars and at the end of the journey or the following morning, always the good smell of the river, as the boy leaned over the bridge to gaze at the grey-backed bleak in shoals of ten or fifteen, swimming idly on the spot: a brackish languor, a hit of something rare, in through the lungs and off through the blood-stream.

As Great West Road people, we never came near Mackenzie Close on our seasonal to-and-fro between London and floodland. Instead of a sobering glimpse of the White City Estate, motorists who preferred the A4 had the frissons of Slough to contend with, a little further out of town. Margaret's territory was hidden from us. But the spirit of the estate would be felt from time to time, along with the spirit of every other big public housing project, as a place where weighty, unanswerable questions might be put about the state of Britain, as though to a vast brick-and-mortar oracle: Who are we? Where are we going? Has public provision been a success or is it preparing people for ever greater dependence on government? Any plan to cater for large numbers of people – people such as Margaret Walsh – sooner or later gave rise to speculation of this kind.

At the junction of Australia Road and Bloemfontein Road I made my way back in the direction I'd come, staying close to the stalwart blocks of housing on my left.

There had been changes in Mackenzie Close since my last visit. Some swings and a slide stood in the centre of the little square where before there'd been an incinerator. I looked up at the door of number 43 and wondered if it could ever have been a shop. Even fifty years ago, and even a small shop: but the structure of the flats wouldn't have allowed for it.

The Westway was rowdier here, as if the close were right up against it. You could glimpse the westbound traffic careering down on to the flat stretch that took it to the first of the big turn-offs for Acton. A constant stream of vehicles hell-for-leathering in the direction of what would soon be sundown.

I walked back east along the Uxbridge Road and into the city, taking the pedestrian underpass at the Shepherds Bush round-about. I made my way up Holland Park Avenue and on to Notting Hill Gate, passing the place where I'd found Maureen and Jill a few years earlier, pretending they were at the seaside. Further along, I passed the Coronet. Inside the cinema Colin's father, a kindly loafer, was helping his only grandson into a seat. The picture was an A certificate with Brigitte Bardot, the year was 1958 or perhaps 1959.

Turning up Hillgate Street, I passed the fish restaurant where I used to go with Maureen once a week in the winter months to eat a mountain of chips and the batter round a large piece of plaice or cod, disdaining the slick white meat. I turned right and up on to Campden Hill Road. The brewery was delivering at the Windsor Castle, where Colin's father used to drink in the late morning, before taking lunch. I went back again down Campden Street looking for Bluebird Cottage, the house where Colin's aunt Phyllis had lived. The façade hadn't really changed. As I looked at the house, Phyllis made a brief appearance. She sat in her armchair with fawn covers lecturing Colin on his waywardness, her head bent by spinal disease. Later there was a small boy reluctantly preparing to give her a kiss somewhere on her grey hair, which she, like Mim, used to keep in a net.

Back on to Campden Hill Road and now across into Airlie Gardens. Making for the end of the little street, past the ungainly brick porches with stuccoed openings, which I used to think of as fortifications.

We'd lived at number 18, winters mostly, until I was seven, I suppose, with Colin's parents upstairs and the unshakeably single Rosemary in a maid's room. The house must have been enormous: it had since been combined with number 17 and converted into flats. I counted nearly twenty buzzers on the intercom. So even if Colin had exaggerated the size of his income in 1952, we'd still have been a family to reckon with, situated in a property of some substance. 'Good care. Baptised.' And a few years later, when Colin had sized things up, come into some of Phyllis's money and settled into a career on the Stock Exchange, we'd have been more or less respectable members of the post-war upper middle class. All this in less than an hour's walk from Mackenzie Close.

The adoption policy that brought down a barrier between the first family and the second, so as to ease the baby into a strange cradle and allay the worries of the mother who'd had to give it up, had much to be said for it. But very few people made the journey between Mackenzie Close and Airlie Gardens in any case. So who needed a barrier?

For a while, I hung about outside the house in the rain. Hadn't there been a tall brick tower on the other side of the road? An old neo-Gothic water tower, quasi-fortified in the style of the porches? If so, it had gone. I'd seemed to remember Colin and Maureen's boy chafing here in the winter weeks, longing for the river, but I wasn't so sure any more. I had a marvellous feeling about the little street, a sense of being rocked between past and present, in a rhythm of constant overlapping and recovery. Like riding a bike along a slow curve in a country road. A limestone wall rises on one side; the wall and the curve seem never to end. But then as they do – as the road digresses from the wall – the pull of the bend is still with you, and the wall is still yours.

On Campden Hill Road, a party of estate agents spilled from the ground-floor showrooms of a large new gated development, speaking with animation into mobile phones. I sensed the flickering presence of the boy I'd been, the only forebear I could really claim, ducking and diving alongside me, as I fought my way through the group of men, clustering like angels, who'd taken possession of the pavement.

That night I dreamed again about Laughing Water, Mim's house by the Loddon. It must have been a variation on the dream I'd failed to remember in the train up to Paris. There was a downpour; the river was a choppy mass of silvery tops with darting spindles of rain. I was inside the house, removing a sticky resin from the keys of the piano, which made no sound, even though I had to press them down to clean them. In the attic room which you reached by the outside staircase, a woman was sleeping. I'd been sent to wake her. She lay on the bed, the lower half of her body covered in a pile of raised material like a tent, and on top of that an off-white mackintosh. Her hair was darkish and short.

Her face was hidden.

By the covers, I'd like to say, though I can't recall.

'It's better if you don't disturb her.'

Downstairs someone asked why I hadn't done as I was told and woken her up. I said: because she was wearing an enormous skirt over a farthingale.

I was standing on the raised concrete walkway with my back to the house. The hoops from the farthingale were trundling slowly through the garden, propelled by the wind in my dream.

VII

People

Peter Privett took my coat and hung it on the back of the front door. In the kitchen he made me tea.

'Are you sure you won't join me for a toasted sandwich?' he asked.

I said I'd wait and he said, after all, he'd wait for a bit himself.

The living room was small and the phone was about where I'd imagined it, though the window gave on to a grass area flanked by other buildings on the estate. There were no cars.

Peter was tall. Good eyes behind the spectacles and strong features. I put him in his mid to late eighties. He showed me a photo of Lilian. She was standing, dressed in a sari – I think he said an Asian friend had shown her how to wear it, and she wore it well. She must have been in her mid-fifties. The photo was taken seven or eight years before she died.

We sat down.

During the war, Peter had been in the air force. He was stationed at Kenley in Surrey and had met Lilian on a night out. She was from Mitcham, a little place near Croydon, once a prosperous village and by the late 1930s a London dormitory. Peter had been posted overseas soon afterwards. They'd corresponded, fallen out, broken it off for a couple of years and finally married after he was demobbed.

The question was how to make a way in civilian life. Peter trained as a decorator, but whatever your earnings in those days, post-war housing was in short supply. He and Lilian camped down in Mitcham with her parents.

It was price instability in confectionery and tobacco that sorted out his life. The fluctuations were so hectic and unpredictable, he said, that British Automatic suspended sales from its vending machines and set up shops instead: Peter and Lilian ran the BA store on Ladbroke Grove – he couldn't quite recall when they took it on – and they had a flat over the shop. That, I said, was where I thought Margaret Walsh might have come in. I sketched a picture of a young girl, very likely Irish, late teens perhaps, a counter assistant of some kind. Maybe she'd worked in the shop, or if she hadn't, maybe she knew someone who did, and she came across Lilian as a result, but Peter thought they'd hired very few staff. Then we went over his wife's role in my story. I explained that I was adopted and how in the court record a Mrs Privett was cited as my adopted mother's cleaning lady – and as the person who'd told her about the unwanted baby, or at any rate the pregnant girl.

That seemed to throw Peter. Lilian had never worked as a cleaning lady – not when they were in Ladbroke Grove. She'd worked with him in the shop. He asked my surname again, and seemed momentarily puzzled that it wasn't Walsh. I reiterated: Walsh was the name of the girl who'd given birth to me, Harding was the name of the adopting couple.

'Well, as I say, she didn't clean for people,' Peter said, 'and we didn't know any Mrs Harding.'

He said he needed time to think about the girl; that the penny might drop. I imagined a padlocked BA vending machine in a railway station a year or two after VE Day.

He started out along what he called 'Irish lines' and yes, he recalled an Irish family up in Kensal Rise, great friends of Lilian's.

'Harriet and Conrad,' he said. 'Their place was full of Irish friends, London Irish and people coming over, looking for work.'

With post-war reconstruction, they were coming in large numbers. But Peter couldn't get a line of thought that led to Margaret.

We went to the kitchen and he put a sandwich in his toaster, battening down the top like a steam-press.

'Old Christie,' Peter said, while we waited for the kettle to boil. 'He was one of our customers.'

'Old Reg Christie.'

'That's the one. Polite chap. If there were girls in the shop, he'd always tip his hat to them, a proper ladies' man. They said he never smoked, but he always bought cigarettes and sweets. Fisherman's bait, if you know what I mean. You used to see him chatting up the half-a-crown types.'

'Half a crown?'

'Girls who'd do it for half a crown. And he used to study the small advertisements in the shop window. He nearly took a flat that way. He asked for the address of the customer who'd placed the card and when I next saw him, I asked: how did you get on? He said he hadn't wanted it. Too many ties, something like that. The last visit he made to the shop, the police were on to him. He didn't seem too ruffled at the time, but that was his way.'

We went back into the living room, armed with coffee and toasted sandwiches. I repeated my surname to Peter, but no lights went on. We were both embarrassed. I spoke about Margaret, and he recalled the name of a woman who'd worked in the shop, but she'd been a Patricia. We talked about tracing family and he said his son was interested in the Privetts. He'd done a bit of work on the genealogy and got as far as some eighteenth-century Privetts in Portsmouth.

'Couldn't go back beyond 1714.'

I could only see that as a resounding success.

We talked about the war. He'd been assigned to the Mediterranean in 1942. There were five thousand men on board his troopship when it was hit by a torpedo off the coast of Algeria. He and his comrades had waited nine hours to be taken off the ship. It blew up twenty minutes after he got to safety. He'd gone on to serve in Tunisia. In 1943 he was on a detail to retrieve ammunition from a British lorry that had crashed near the Algerian border. On the way back they were shot up by a fighter plane; he was out of action for several months. He recovered and went on to fight on Sardinia and the Italian mainland. I knew the Algerian-Tunisian border a little and we spoke about the bright, thankless terrain away from the coast; it was something we had in common.

What became of Lilian, I wondered, once they'd left the shop in Ladbroke Grove?

She'd taken up administrative work with social services, he

said, and he'd remained a shopkeeper, running a series of franchises all over south London – that was their real home, he added, not Ladbroke Grove, not the west.

Peter's eyesight was failing now, but he was a keen painter. He had a stout portfolio and showed me his portraits of Lilian, some careful landscapes he'd done in Surrey, some movie queens, including Marilyn – and a virtuoso painting of oast houses in Kent, which I admired so much that he gave it to me.

'By way of not being able to help you,' he said, adjusting his weight in the chair and showing signs of early afternoon fatigue.

We wrapped the picture and I got up to go.

I'd planted Margaret's name in this unpromising soil. There was vigour in it yet, and there might be a result.

It was fine, he said, to ring in a couple of days. Age did odd things to your memory and he said again that he needed time. We passed Lilian, the beautiful older woman in the sari. I got my coat from the back of the door.

'Adoption's a hard one to fathom,' Peter said. 'You'll need a bit of luck if you really mean to find anything out.'

I could hear a plaintive sigh from the sleeping dogs that Boris had urged me to let lie.

Peter was holding the painting while I dug a space for it in my bag.

'Lilian had a great friend,' he said, in a rambling, nice-to-have-met-you way. 'It was years ago. A friend from the old days, before Ladbroke Grove – and she adopted a little boy. Anyway, it was all a secret because evidently they were worried he wouldn't . . . apparently they thought if anyone found out, he'd never be one of the new family. They were wealthy, you see, and the thing was . . . they thought that if it got out in the open, he'd never settle or inherit any money. So it was a . . . they did it on the quiet.'

He raised his eyebrows.

'Well,' I suggested, 'that's one way of doing it. It's not the thing nowadays.'

'We never knew how it worked out,' said Peter, bending to swat at a trace of toasted sandwich on the hem of his cardigan. 'Because you see, Maureen – that was the name of Lilian's friend – she'd have nothing to do with us after that.'

Peter led the way back into the living room as I tried to understand how the adoption barrier had failed to come down properly, how the firewall had contained a vent, or the lock gates had sprung a leak. I thought I had an inkling, but I couldn't quite get to it and now I took my place on the sofa again, and Peter asked wouldn't I like to take my coat off.

'You see, Maureen and Lilian,' he said, 'they were very good friends. They'd grown up on the same street, practically, in council housing in Mitcham. Everyone knew each other – that sort of thing. Well, I'd not met Lilian at the time, it was before the war, but evidently Maureen married an extremely wealthy man and she got off the estate, didn't she?'

'That was Graham she married.'

'That was Graham of course – and Graham and Maureen had two children, I knew that from Lilian. Then after the war – well, I mean in the 1950s – they must have wanted a third and I don't know why they'd have wanted to adopt – but I suppose that's how they came to have you. Meanwhile, you see, my wife must have known about this Irish girl – your real mother – or you, or . . . and she'd have told Maureen . . .'

Peter ran out of steam and we sized each other up with cheerful amazement as Lilian stood in her sari looking on.

'Well, I'm blowed,' he said. 'If I hadn't come up with her name, you'd have been out that door and you'd have been none the wiser.'

He removed his spectacles, examined them at arm's length and replaced them.

In a moment, he'd settled a lifetime of vague perplexities on my part about Maureen. Indeed, he'd explained her very well. And in return I began supplying the fragments of the picture he hadn't known.

'You see, Maureen didn't stay with Graham.'

'She didn't?' He looked puzzled and obscurely upset.

'No,' I said, 'she went off with a man called Colin. Colin Harding.'

'When was that?'

'Well, I suppose that was around 1950.'

'You've thrown me there,' he said. 'How on earth? Graham was so generous to her, wasn't he, and she had everything . . . everything you could possibly . . . I mean, coming from the estate in Mitcham and her being set up in a place like that. Did you ever see Graham's house in Caterham?'

I envisaged a very large house with a good many guest rooms. And I saw a Sunday breakfast with Graham, Maureen, Colin and Boris – and the staff hovering near the scullery. A row of expensive cars in the drive.

'In any case,' I went on, 'she divorced Graham and married the new fellow, and she'd been ill, you know, she'd had TB, I think it was. Whatever it was, she didn't want more children, or she couldn't have them, but Colin, my father – my adoptive father – he did want children of his own, so to speak. Which is how they must have hit on adoption. And that's where Lilian came in – and Margaret Walsh. And me.'

Peter was quiet for a moment. He was going back over the story.

'So,' he said, 'I'll just get it straight. You're Maureen's boy. Maureen's adopted boy. You're the boy I talked about when we were standing in the hallway just now. But you're not Graham's adopted boy because she'd already left Graham when she got you.'

'That's it,' I said.

Peter looked tired again, but intrigued and faintly amused. He cast a glance out of the window at the grass and the pale rendering on the wall of the block a few yards away.

'Tell me about the money,' I asked, 'and the thing about, you know, their worry that the boy wouldn't be . . . accepted.' I had a vision of an early breakthrough with organ transplants.

'Well, you tell me,' he replied with a laugh. 'I mean, I'd always understood Maureen had adopted the boy while she was with Graham. And . . . what with Graham being a millionaire . . . but

Maureen's new husband . . . your father . . . was there quite a lot of money there?'

'They were comfortable,' I said. 'Colin hadn't much money at the time, but he and Maureen lived in a house with his parents, and there was money around. No one was going to starve.'

'But nothing like Graham's money.'

'Nothing like Graham's.'

'I mean, Maureen, dear old Maureen,' he said, 'I wouldn't . . . I mean, I hope you see my point: she went from rags to riches when she married Graham.'

I didn't doubt it.

Peter rose to his feet.

'Graham kept a lot of cars. He had a Packard and she got her driving licence thanks to him, and he let her drive it. She used to take Lilian out in the Packard during the war. They called it motoring in those days. And here,' he said, beckoning me into the hallway. 'Maureen gave us this.'

There was a fine antique mirror in a gilded wooden frame mounted opposite the front door.

In the early days, after the war but before Lilian and Peter moved to Ladbroke Grove, the new couple in Caterham used to drive over to Mitcham. Graham and Maureen and Maureen's old friends would go to the pub, and a few of those same friends would be asked up to the big house from time to time. Caterham wasn't far from Mitcham, except in terms of class and income, and Graham had a way of taking the larger sorts of distance in his stride.

Peter looked at his watch. He said, 'You know who might be able to help you is Lilian's brother Bert.'

'He's still alive?'

I was thinking of Margaret.

'Oh yes,' said Peter, 'he's not far from Mitcham. Sutton, Surrey. Morden's the nearest tube. He's younger than Lilian – younger than she'd have been now. Bert knew Maureen well, in the old days anyway. And of course he grew up on the estate in Mitcham. But whether that'll help you with your . . . what was her name?'

Yes, he'd spoken to Bert.

'Only I forgot to tell you, he likes to be called John nowadays. No more Bert.'

I asked how Bert, or John, had reacted.

'No objections to talking to you. None at all.'

I thanked Peter again for his Kentish landscape. I was about to send it home by mail.

Morden felt like the wrong direction. Off the beat. The beat was supposed to be westerly, and Morden was southerly. Still, I'd had the same discouraging feeling about Arnos Grove and now I struck out against the current with very little trouble.

By Morden station I bought a pot plant and a dessert wine, crossed the road and waited for the 93 bus.

Until the age of forty or so, when I'd become a father, there'd never been any question of a family likeness between me and another person, and I'd had only a few years practice in the arts of physical comparison based on kinship. It was therefore a little silly to ask myself whether John Webb looked like me, but I could still say with a measure of certainty that he had a resemblance about the upper part of the face to two of my three sons. I'd seen it when Peter showed me the photos and I'd thought about it since – to my middle son especially. But the boy was only seven and I didn't trust what I'd seen. Besides, he looked like his mother, not me.

The Webb establishment was a big detached house, faux Tudor, forty or fifty years old, with a black cab – he'd alerted me to that – parked out front in the little drive.

John Webb was a very focused man. You saw it right away in the eyes, and the laughter lines at their edges. The cheekbones seemed more pronounced for the silvery sideburns, longer than you'd find in most men of his age – about ten years younger, I reckoned, than Peter Privett. There was no bridge to the nose. It came straight down from the forehead taking an elegant curve at the last moment. But for that curve, he might have been a boxer in his youth: there was a discreet flattening of the features, especially

105

the top lip. But the bottom lip was full and the chin was strong. The build was slight. I could see the young soldier in uniform in the 1940s.

He put the wine in the fridge. His wife took the plant and announced that she was going out for a while. I told him what he already knew about my meeting with Peter Privett. He watched me, nodding as I went. Then there was Margaret Walsh, but instead we slid around quickly to the subject of Maureen.

Some of the ground had been covered by Peter, but there were new details. As a boy, John had looked up to Maureen – she was his big sister's friend and when she'd left the estate to go off with Graham, he'd been pleased to see her come back from time to time. He knew her as his Auntie Maureen. With the marriage to Graham, there had been a change of Eliza-like proportions. Graham had paid for her to have elocution lessons, John said, and classes in deportment. She'd once appeared in *Vogue* or the *Tatler*, he didn't recall. He remembered her coming to pick him up in the Packard – him and Lilian. They'd driven into town and had tea at a Lyons Corner House. She'd left half a crown on the table and John, or Bert as he was, had pointed it out as they got up to go, but his Auntie Maureen was tipping lavishly by then.

'What my brother-in-law hadn't realised when he spoke to you', John said, 'was that Maureen had left Graham. We never got wind of it.'

His voice was controlled; the old Mitcham accent had been neutralised by time and evidently by prosperity.

I asked when he'd last had anything to do with Maureen, and he told me that some time in 1950 or not long after, his mother and Lilian had been forbidden to see her. This 'forbidden' was familiar. It had Colin all over it.

'That was her new husband,' I said.

'I suppose that's right,' John said.

'But she must have told Lilian that they weren't to see one another any more, and in that case, Lilian would have known that Maureen was no longer with Graham.'

'I think she probably did know. But she didn't bother telling

Peter, and I wasn't around much at the time. Or it's possible she mentioned it and we got the wrong end of the stick. I mean, all I knew was that we weren't to see Maureen any more, so it didn't really matter where she was or who she was with. Although it wasn't like Graham to do that kind of thing. Not in his nature.'

'Wasn't it hard not to see her again?' I asked.

'Very hard for Lilian,' he said, 'but by then there'd been the war, and one thing and another. People went their own ways.'

And what of Colin's character? Was he a likeable man? I said he was the person I thought of as my father, and I watched John Webb very closely.

'Well, that's right,' he said.

There was nothing, not a flicker, from the former Merchant Navy steward.

I told him what I thought had happened to Maureen's social standing after she left Graham and how precarious Colin's life as a stockbroker had been after the war. I said what a good bridge player he was and that this had added to their income in the early days; how he'd depended on his parents for a flat near Notting Hill Gate; how his aunt had begun to help him once I'd come into the picture; how that had enabled them to get a place of their own in London in 1960 or so. I explained that Graham and Colin remained friends despite the business with Maureen, but that Maureen used to regret the ease and gaiety of the years in Caterham.

John Webb went out to put the kettle on.

I felt suddenly very blue about Maureen, sad about her life, as I might have felt, but hadn't, when she died.

When he returned, we chatted respectfully about her for a little longer, breaking off to sip from the tea or coffee, whatever it was, like masons pausing to inspect their work on a monument. In memoriam. Maureen in Mitcham. Maureen in Caterham. Maureen at a Lyons Corner House. And for my own part, in private: Maureen in the christening photo of her third child, outside St Mary Abbots – the powdered face, which men found so fetching, riven by her smile, less like a pantomime rat now and more like the face of a pierrot, or a picture-book moon, beaming above the porky, disgruntled baby. Then Maureen the flower girl. Maureen the upper-order lady with the upper-order voice. Maureen well away, flat out on the floor of the living room with her glass lying by the armchair. Maureen in her old people's home, all but inert. Maureen's send-off at the crematorium, the floodwater almost up to the cloister.

'She turned out', I said, 'to be a very talented florist. A real flair for arrangements.'

'When was that?' he asked.

'In the 1960s,' I said. 'She had a shop – for several years. She was happy. She made her own money. It was a new lease of life.'

'What happened to all that?'

I remembered the arguments with Colin in the flat upstairs.

'That was another thing that ended up being forbidden.'

John Webb inspected his hands.

I wondered if he knew how Graham and Maureen had met. He didn't, but he thought maybe she'd been working in a restaurant where Graham used to go for meals, or a shop where he used to call by. But no, not really: it was just one of those startling encounters that should have become legendary and didn't – and it had led to a rather startling marriage.

He was right, wasn't he, to assume that Maureen was no longer alive? What had become of her?

I mentioned she'd been lost in space for a while before her death.

'Ah yes,' said John.

'Probably on account of the drink,' I said.

'I see,' he said.

If he'd loved his Auntie Maureen, John had thought the world of her first husband. Like Peter, he spoke of Graham getting into one of the cars with Maureen – 'even the Roller' – to drive to Mitcham and take her old friends down the pub. He told me that Graham had got him out of factory work in his early teens and given him odd jobs at the big house. That was during the war. Lilian, too, had earned a bit of money in Caterham – perhaps the citation in the court records, describing her as 'Mrs Harding's ex-char lady', had a grain of truth. It would have been a strange relationship for as long as it lasted.

Many of Maureen's mannerisms, her airs, had been a bit dubious. Sometimes the accent was overdone – Shaw would have called it 'sham golfing English'. Maybe John agreed?

'Whenever my mother – our mother – went to visit in Caterham,' John said, 'Maureen's accent rubbed off on her and she'd come home a little posher than she'd left. I mean, we weren't posh, you know, and nor was Maureen in the old days. So Lilian and I used to take the mickey out of our mother. But Maureen? No. She changed herself about a bit, fixed herself up – or Graham fixed her up – and she managed it well, I thought. Graces, yes, but not too many airs. Imagine a girl from a council-house family marrying into a world like Graham's. You have to be a good mixer to pull that off, and she did, you see.'

As John spoke, I could see my mother – Mother Two – shimmying along the barrows in Covent Garden, with the lights on over the winter pinks in their raked boxes: not yet dawn in London, cups of tea in the cold with the market traders, everything coming on Christmas, a bit of banter. 'Nice to meet your boy, Mrs H.' And to me: 'She's a lovely lady, your mother.'

But I wanted to get closer to Margaret now, and in view of the suspicions I had, that meant closer to John. I wasn't sure how to go about it, and began with the photos from his soldiering days.

John had enlisted in the army in 1945. He was eighteen. He'd been shipped to Egypt for eight months, and then to Palestine. They'd assigned him to Haifa and he'd made the most of it. You looked at John and you could see that wherever he'd been, whatever he'd done, he'd always meant to have a good time, and girls – you could tell this too – were a good time. So yes, he found a Jewish girlfriend on a kibbutz near his battalion quarters. She'd been run off the kibbutz when the headmen discovered she was consorting with a British soldier. Not long afterwards, a group of Jewish militants mined the road. John's vehicle was blown up; he was thrown clear by the blast, and recovered after a few weeks in hospital.

When he came out of the army, he enrolled for training as a leatherworker. For a time, he worked as a supplier of leg-irons and callipers, travelling around clinics, measuring and fitting for disabled people. He'd been happy then, too. Even so, he'd changed tack and gone into the Merchant Navy. He was hazy about the dates. It was 1949 or 1950 perhaps when he was out in Ceylon and had news that his father was dying. Getting home was impossible. There was no money. But then he was told that a ticket had been paid for and he'd be flown out of Colombo within a few days. He discovered later that Graham had put up the money.

'That was Graham for you,' he said.

John left the Merchant Navy a couple of years later, and he didn't see Maureen again, but he saw Lilian. She was in Ladbroke Grove with Peter by that time.

'Which is where I think Margaret Walsh comes into it,' I suggested. 'There's a connection with Lilian.'

'Yes,' John said. It was a circumspect 'yes', qualified by a short sigh – and then, after a pause: 'I saw the young girl about twice.'

I kept my eyes trained on him and I think he knew what I might be thinking. He was impassive. It was those Irish friends of Lilian's, he went on. Her name was Harriet – the surname was Buggle, something like that – and a man called Conrad. 'Nice people.'

Peter had mentioned them, I said.

'Well, I met her up there,' he said. 'At their place in Kensal Rise.'

'You were on leave in London?'

'Yes, on leave, or just out of the navy for good, I forget.'

'It must be hard to remember,' I said, 'and it's a stupid question to ask you half a century later . . .' It was John's turn to study me now. '. . . but what was she like?'

'Well, Harriet and Conrad, they were lively, very sociable, and the place was often full of people, so I mean, I scarcely noticed her. She was . . . she was very young. And, as far as I could tell, she was very shy.'

I asked what she looked like.

'She was southern Irish,' he said, 'a country girl, you know. Very provincial. Naïve and likeable. I had the impression she'd

110

only just arrived. I can't honestly remember how she looked. Yes, I'm sure she was likeable.'

We glanced at one another, John on one side of the sofa with a table lamp beside him, me in an armchair, at right angles to him, with a good view of his profile. I adjusted my posture slightly, to fix him from a different position. Again I tried to see if there was anyone he looked like.

'You see,' he said, 'I can tell you more about Maureen than I can about your . . . about the girl at Harriet and Conrad's all those years ago. For your purposes, I'm a Maureen buff. Well,' he laughed, 'not even that.'

When his wife came back, I drank more tea and he showed me some photos of the cars he'd bought over the years.

'Maureen started my addiction to cars,' he said.

He'd worked hard in the rag trade and life had turned very sweet in the 1960s. He pointed to a picture of his daughter by an earlier marriage and I scanned it for resemblances to my sons. Then he drove me up to Morden station in his black cab – an irresistible addition, he told me, to his car collection.

I asked him to think about Margaret. Should anything occur to him, well, I'd be in touch anyway, if he had no objection.

'None at all,' he said.

On the stairs down to the platform at Morden station, I began composing the letter I'd write him, inquiring whether he was my father.

VIII

Honours

The night was muggy. I lay in bed, unable to listen to the news on the radio. The voices bustled from the set and fell to an unceremonious death somewhere by the counterpane I'd set in a heap on the floor.

Too much was happening on the inside, as it were, in the opaque realms of my own feelings, where I'd hoped to discover a sort of softening towards Colin and Maureen. Looking for Margaret had meant thinking about them often, and I'd begun to hope I could give them their freedom, let them loose in my mind's eye and relearn the primitive affection I'd felt for them when I was a boy. They were dead, it was late in the day, but I'd grown fonder of Maureen now that I knew about her in a way I hadn't before. The story of Colin's forbidding – which I recognised clearly – was a setback, however, and in approaching the man I suspected was my father by blood, I'd drawn close to the memory of Colin again, only to find that my opinion of him was, if anything, lower than it had been when he was alive.

Why was this exactly? For a while – a dangerous phase, I'd say now – I'd been flattered by the fact that I was adopted, and therefore unusual, but I'd never believed in a special connection between a father and his genetic son of which I'd been deprived: at the time I was a boy and later an adolescent, people weren't saying that kind of thing within earshot and I'd never have dreamed it up myself. As a child I could smell Colin and hold him, as I could Maureen, which had been good enough. So it must be the case, I reasoned, that I'd found a new pretext to punish him for ground we'd already been over when I was a hostile, clever teenager who'd disparaged his way of thinking, his heroes, his politics and his way of life.

Even so, the fact that Colin had forbidden Lilian and John, and presumably their mother, to see Maureen was objectionable. Colin hated the idea of a jumbled, classless society and if Maureen had made herself over, with the help of Graham, to become an attractive example of the better class of person, there'd be no backsliding on her part for as long as Colin had anything to do with it. He might have a sympathetic chuckle at Eliza Doolittle's father – they were both idlers – but he wasn't going to have that sort of character in the house.

But then the way the adoption was arranged meant that there'd not been a proper slamming and bolting of doors between the baby's provenance and its future. Things had been done by word of mouth, thanks largely to Maureen's ability to move back and forth across the class divide and to her friendship with Lilian. And after Colin and Maureen had got their boy, it had been time to put an end to her agility. Unless she was barred from her own past, their boy might have been accessible to his own.

No one in social services could have done that. Nothing in the adoption file suggested that the child welfare officer or the child protection visitor had an indication of Maureen's background. How were they to know that the ex-'char lady' of the elegant divorcee they'd interviewed was one of her closest friends? So it fell to Colin to cloister his son from the confusion that might result if Lilian or John, or any of Maureen's people from Mitcham, visited the house – John, above all, I found myself thinking – and to ensure that the secret was less likely to get out.

True. But it came naturally to Colin to forbid. Would Graham have issued the order so easily and painlessly? Colin, who allowed himself all sorts of latitude, was in general keen to rein in other people. In our various places by the river, he was always chasing walkers away – 'It's clearly marked! Private!' – or accosting drivers who strayed on to our unremarkable, remote gravel track: 'This is a private road and if you don't turn back this instant, I shall call the police!' (Officers of the state might be invoked on the proper occasions.) The few neighbours we had were not like this with strangers. But Colin didn't approve of neighbours either.

Both he and Maureen were heavy drinkers. He was good at

drinking and she was not. When Maureen's drinking got out of hand in the 1960s, Colin made an effort to reduce his intake. The idea was to support her, and to applaud the daring posture she'd assumed, like a girl in a Wild West show, half on the wagon, half off. But before too long Colin returned to his steady rate and forbade her to drink at most times of day – at eleven on a Saturday morning, for example, as he helped himself to his first scotch and water.

'I'm afraid you'll have to wait. Can I get you a lime juice and tonic?'

'But how will I cook the lunch without a little pick-me-up?'

In due course, she became militant and he settled for lofty resignation; there are plenty of husbands who thrive on feeling let down by their wives.

Whenever I caught a glimpse of this disheartening state of affairs – whenever I was home from school – the water seemed to have risen a few more feet, leaving a little less ground for my diminutive, disappointed parents to occupy. I used to cheer up Maureen by preparing tonic in an arcane soda-maker that resembled a small artillery piece.

'Thank you, sweetie, thank you so much. You'll make the perfect bartender when we've had your sticky-out teeth done. Where's your father?'

And under her grateful eye, with Colin at the far end of the garden, I'd add a conspiratorial dash of gin to her glass.

If he was good at denying Maureen what she wanted, Colin was rarely satisfied by his own freedoms. Perversely, though he began to do better in the City, and kept a level income from the bridge tables, and embarked on a decade of successful property speculation, the pressure of wanting more, but not quite getting it, offset the benefits of his new-found prosperity. In its alluring way, the feeling of entitlement – pretension rather than ambition – kept one step ahead of expenditure. A complex set of counterweights had begun to restrain the generosity of which he was capable.

He was also undergoing a radical awakening: a revolution of attitude as heady as anything the younger generation lived through in the 1960s, and probably a greater force for change. It was the emergence of asset-stripping as a quick way to make money that won him over – and the people who brought this game to the City, a game which respected none of the old rules and certainly not the old money, became his idols. Slater Walker Securities Ltd was Colin's favourite subject of conversation, while Slater Walker's 'industrial group', which specialised in aggressive takeovers, followed by rapid sell-offs and steep rises in share values, was possibly his favourite recommendation to clients, now that beige suitcases were a thing of the past. And Jim Slater was his man. Colin had seen the future: it owed nobody anything, it was astute, iconoclastic, crassly self-interested – and it worked. His enthusiasm for the new moguls jeopardised Colin's stubborn independence of mind, his shrewdness, even his bigotry. Whenever we got around to talking – an activity that could end badly for us in the late 1960s – I felt stunned, like a parent whose child has collapsed into the arms of a religious cult.

That feeling was probably wrong. Until the undoing of Slater Walker in 1974, Colin's loyalties were not entirely clear. He was in thrall to Jim Slater and the pirate following that Slater inspired, but he kept a sentimental attachment to the Establishment ways that his new heroes – James Hanson and James Goldsmith among them by now – were busy dismantling. After a time, the character of money, how it was made and who'd made it, mattered less to him than money as such. Yet however well he did, he seemed obscurely disappointed and in the 1970s his sense that he deserved better grew more marked. Somehow the world had failed to come up to scratch. If something wasn't good enough for Lord Lucan or Lord Someone Else, on the one hand, or Jimmy Goldsmith on the other – the kinds of people he was meeting at the bridge table – then it would never do for him. But the more Colin struck off his list, with his no to this person and no to the other, or take this away to the head waiter, or get off my property this instant, the more robustly life seemed to repay him in kind. It was always a risk that Colin's high opinion of himself and his hankering for the 'exclusive' life would leave him marooned and excluded – and with no more than a handful of friends by the end.

But his toughest exclusionary swipe was administered at home. It had taken Maureen three or four years to get the flower shop off the ground and it took about three months for him to close her down, once he'd decided he'd have no more of it. The accounts were poorly kept and he hadn't liked that; there were debts unpaid and he hadn't liked that; she was too busy to cook and clean for him and he hadn't liked that. Finally, she invited some of the market traders from Covent Garden to our house on the Thames – a dreary modern bungalow set on a brick course had now replaced the old houseboat – where they could spend the morning angling and she could make them lunch. Colin was angry.

'But they're my friends,' she'd protested, 'and they're fishermen. It only seems fair to let them come and sit by the river. I never use it. I hate it.'

'I don't care whether they're fishermen or camel-herders,' he'd told her.

Within a year she'd sold the business, to stay on as a part-time hand; not long afterwards, the Eliza Doolittle thing was finished entirely.

The morning was brighter than usual. I turned away from it and sank my face back in the pillow. It smelled of Colin. Tobacco on skin. I saw a marbling of intense colours: emeralds and dark blues; a bright, mamba green, flush with a lustrous orange. The colours began to seethe, and then resolved into stripes – why that?

I'd emerged from the night with a glassy, muddled retrospect of Colin's service medals, as if they'd been the last images in a dream otherwise lost in the waking. I suppose it must have been the stories of Peter's war and John Webb's that had prompted this march-past of Colin's: he'd been in Italy and Greece for some of the time. And the medals? He'd given them to me, one by one, event by event, for boyish stoicism in the face of various mishaps – measles, sunburn, a barefoot stroll by a wasps' nest.

There were five or six – campaign medals for the most part, with oak leaves on two.

I clambered into my clothes, thinking of Colin in the old days: laughing with friends, doing the rounds – 'let me top you up' – talking money with a partner who'd come over for lunch at the weekend. Then I was at the stern of a dinghy as he took us briskly down river and moored. I saw him toss away the end of his cigarette, heard the fup as it hit the water, watched it bobbing briefly. The two of us went into the village to do the shopping.

I found myself mourning the easygoing figure who'd stood at the edge of my childhood. A man who enjoyed little children, including his boy: I'd understood, later on, how Peter's family, and Jill's, could breathe life back into him as they charged around the house on visits during the 1960s. A man whose vanity was only exceeded by his charm and the quantity of cigarettes he smoked. I liked this person better than the person he became. Though I owed Colin everything, or a very great deal, I wanted the debt inscribed with the image of the younger man. The one coming through the door of the flat in London, removing his bowler hat and laying aside a furled umbrella, as I ran to greet him. Or the one in the kitchen on New Year's Eve, settling ice around a bottle in an aluminium bucket.

Blood had nothing to do with it. Families worked or they didn't. It was all in the way you handled it. A father couldn't choose his son, and a son couldn't choose his father.

Even so, I must have been making some kind of choice as I went down to the kitchen, switched on the kettle and began my letter to John Webb.

The rain was clattering on Hammersmith.

The librarian in charge of the Lilla Huset archives hadn't expected anything quite so waterlogged in the reading room and looked me up and down with dismay. She had the files that would interest me, she said, but I might like to dry off first. In the lavatories, I disabled the brake on the miserly toilet-roll dispenser and yanked out a turban's length of paper, wrapped it round my head and sat for a minute or two, occasionally wringing out the turn-ups on my trousers.

The library kept documents on the administrative history of Hammersmith and Fulham. It also held books and assorted materials about the social history of the area, including copious press clippings from which I'd requested a sample about the White City Estate. It was obvious from a preliminary trawl through the clippings that over the years reporters had let the place lie until an incident brought them in to get a story. In the intervals there were earnest puffs about well-being and community.

In the late 1980s, nearly ninety per cent of the residents believed that the estate had a bad image. About sixty per cent thought this was 'unfair', and were 'very or fairly' satisfied with their lives. A few years later, the estate got a facelift, and then there'd been a downturn. Nowadays it was thought to be a bit shabby and criminalised, a touch down at heel, a habitat for single-parent families, asylum seekers, that kind of thing. How many people lived there? The various figures averaged out at a little less than three thousand. It was a population in decline.

The clippings produced the same effect on me as any sort of printed ephemera had when I was a boy. Like the comics I used to read, the bits of newspaper spread in front of me opened on to an 'out there' which was full of promise. But the estate itself, in this random accumulation of stories, also spoke of something I'd been brought up at school to think of, almost in defiance of poor Colin and Maureen, as the public imagination: a way of recognising people's needs, even if these were not, or no longer, your own.

From a couple of the older documents set out by the librarian, I learned that in making my way around the White City Estate, I'd been pacing out the lineaments of what had once been a large pleasure park next to the site of the Olympic Games of 1908. The park was designed for a Franco-British exhibition in the same year. The idea was to reaffirm the Entente Cordiale between France and Britain and to bring the French president of the day to London, five years after Edward VII had made his state visit to Paris.

The exhibition was a fantastic concoction of colonial exoticism on the one hand, and indigenous science and industry on the other. There were forty acres of buildings, including eight halls each measuring 400 feet by seventy. A hundred acres of the site were given over to gardens; there was half a mile of artificial waterway. A vast Court of Honour was erected on a fake lagoon dotted with pillared bridges and piers. Plaster-clad follies with latticed windows were set on stilts protruding from the water.

The styles were mid-imperial, British and French, a hodge-podge of Ceylonese and Siamese, Mogul and Chinoiserie. There were 'Algerian gardens' and an 'Irish village'. With all the stucco, it had the look of a white city – which is how the place got its name. By the end of the year, both the exhibition site and the Olympic stadium had served their purpose. Britain had won more than fifty gold medals in the games.

Many of the buildings came down after the exhibition, and what was left of the White City became a public entertainment. You could still go on an extraordinary ride known as the Flip-Flap, with two mobile arms, like a gigantic jousting dummy. At the end of each arm, 150 feet long, was a cage. For a halfpenny you could travel in one of the cages with more than twenty other passengers, as the arms moved slowly up and down. Or you could walk with your family the length of a canal. But within a few years, you'd have seen deep fissures in the stucco and weeds in the desiccated waterways. The exhibition site fell into disrepair. The Olympic stadium was turned over to greyhound racing in 1927, but the decaying amenity near by had long since ceased to serve any purpose.

In 1936 a survey of the Metropolitan boroughs and the City of London found them to contain more than 70,000 overcrowded dwellings. Under slum clearance, more than half were earmarked for demolition. In the same year, the London County Council's purchase order for fifty acres of the exhibition site was confirmed by the courts. It was thought that the estate might house as many as ten or eleven thousand people in '2,150 self-contained flats'. Hard to see Margaret's ancestors walking in the remains of the

'Irish village', but a young Irish girl serving in a shop in Mackenzie Close by the end of the war was not a far-fetched idea.

By 1939, with a good part of the building work done, the estate was hailed by the *West London Observer* as 'a venture that must excite the dullest imagination'. The paper called it 'the most gigantic housing effect ever achieved by any municipality in the world', and the figures were now more specific: 11,000 people would have homes.

The war held up the resettlement of Londoners – and it seems to have held up the last of the building work, but as people started moving in, the *Times* reported that the weekly rental for a family unit would be about seven shillings. Another article put it at five and sixpence a week with an extra shilling for a gas refrigerator. Which made Colin Harding's £1,200 a year, true or not, look like a tidy sum.

IX

Margaret

Kensington Library had supplied a list of voters in Chesterton Road fifty years ago. The remaining business at the Lilla Huset archive was to look at the electoral rolls in White City and establish who'd lived in Mackenzie Close after the war. There were a fair few Walshes in and around the estate at the time and altogether a good many Irish families, flesh-and-blood inheritors of the ersatz Irish village. Kennealies, McNallies, Fosters, Sullivans, Dolans, O'Sheas, Connors, Donovans, Cooles. But there were no Walshes in Mackenzie Close at the end of the 1940s.

Number 43 itself looked very much like an ordinary flat in the close rather than a shop. Until 1950 it was occupied by the Carpenter family, and then in 1951 by a Kathleen and William Hannafin, presumably Irish. They were still there in 1952, the year I was born.

The list of retailers in the area might contain a Chain Stores. There was a wine seller; a 'Dining Rooms' run by Mrs Daisy Griffiths. There were drapers, boot repairers, butchers and 'French cleaners', but the nearest thing to a shop of the kind I'd imagined Margaret working in was 'Jas. Thos. Barrett, Greengrocer'. It was not in Mackenzie Close. I began to think there'd never been a shop at number 43. Or that if there had, it was run as a sideline from the flat, by the Hannafins for instance. But why call it 'Chain Stores'? You might as well call your apartment on the estate 'Hammersmith Lodge'.

I returned to the electoral rolls, in the hope that Margaret had been staying with the Hannafins at number 43, or even living with them, but had been too young to vote at the time she gave birth.

She did not appear in 1953. Instead Kathleen and William Hannafin were joined by an Edward Stephen Walshe – a special mark by his name showed that he was in the services. The discovery of the name, even with the variant spelling, felt briefly like a momentous advance: this person would have to be related to Margaret. By the following year E. S. Walshe had disappeared from the roll. It was no great loss, however, for the Hannafins were now to be seen alongside Margaret Walshe.

It was the first time I'd read the name Margaret Walsh, except on my birth certificate, without wondering whether it was the right Margaret Walsh. I was sure of it. I looked at it for some time, ruminating on the 'e'. Not much there to dent my confidence: the rolls and registers were full of anomalies.

It makes sense, after a piece of good fortune like this, to keep going forward year by year through the electoral rolls until the name of the person you're looking for disappears, and if it's a young woman – in the 1950s anyhow – you can return to the marriage registers with that year in view, advancing quarter by quarter until you come across her, or you don't. Alternatively, you may assume that her name never changed by marriage and look for her in the register of deaths.

I moved with superstitious caution to the 1954 roll and found her again, with her extra 'e'. I swayed nervously from 1954 to 1955, like someone crossing a ravine by a rope bridge. She was still there. From the safety of 1955, I slid quickly off a rock ledge and took 1956 by surprise. Still there. I crossed the open ground to 1957 at a loping pace. The Hannafins remained where they were – I tried to visualise the kitchen – but Margaret was gone.

I made a hasty note of the neighbours' names. Wests at number 41. McCarthys at 44. Palfreys at 40. It would be easier, I guessed on my way out of the library, to find the right Hannafins than it would be to find the Walshes. Hannafin was an unusual name – and so was Palfrey. Hannafin and Palfrey might be the way forward. I couldn't tell.

It was a cold, beautiful night. I imagined Reginald Christie making his last appearance in Peter and Lilian's shop, with a faint smell of Tommy Brock about him, and buying a tin of violet breath-fresheners. I hoped, too, that this was his last appearance in the spectral retinue I'd acquired as I'd gone about the city. I hadn't much enjoyed his company: to think about a murderer is to imagine oneself worse than one is – or at least to ask why one's fallen in with that kind of low life. His crimes, I found, were less troubling than the change he'd wrought in the moral character and eventually the physiognomy of a neighbourhood. Chesterton Road and Mackenzie Close were still on the map, holding out dimly for continuity. But the fate of Rillington Place suggested that fifty years was too long for minor information, of the kind I was after, to survive in London: both the addresses I had to go on were to that extent already rubble in my mind's eye. And there'd be no extricating Margaret Walsh, I felt. Not so much as an earring.

How easy would it be for John Webb to pick up the phone and speak to someone who'd lately written to accuse him of jumping into bed with Margaret Walsh fifty years earlier? Accused was too strong. I might be having to blunder about, but I prided myself on my delicacy. The gist of the letter was that I'd be grateful if he could remember anything else about the girl he'd met at Harriet and Conrad's. Even trifling things. Colour of eyes or hair. Vivacious or dull. Whatever he recalled her saying.

Maureen, the letter went on, had always spoken of the natural father as a waiter, or steward, in the Merchant Navy, and didn't he agree that this was a coincidence? It would be a relief to think that he, John, was my father, because in that case, there'd be no need to pursue the matter.

I hoped the letter had given John Webb the impression I liked him, because I did, very much. Still, whatever the tone of a letter like that, you wouldn't hasten to the phone the moment you'd read it. You'd want to mull it over, especially if you were John Webb. Careful, that's to say, even a little on his guard. Yet for the next two or three days, I continued in the hope that he'd soon be in touch.

Meanwhile there were more letters to be written. A good number, in fact, for despite Margaret's appearance in Mackenzie Close, it seemed foolish to rule out a possible connection with Chesterton Road. I put the names I'd come across in the electoral rolls – possible neighbours in Kensington and Hammersmith half a century ago – into an internet search site and asked it for matches. A stroke of luck might produce one such neighbour, or a neighbour's descendant, a son or daughter. Families might have kept in touch even though they no longer lived in the same street, and children often remembered their parents' friends.

I began with names culled from the Kensington rolls: Walkers, Drakes, Baileys, a Diana Burton. On the website, there were thirty or forty matching names at various addresses around Britain in 2001. I narrowed them down to about ten and drafted letters asking if they'd lived in Chesterton Road during the 1950s.

Then the names associated with Mackenzie Close: I'd already found living Palfreys and McCarthys and shortlisted half a dozen. I'd done the same with Hannafins, Hanafins, Hanifins and Hannifins. Of these, there were eight or nine who might have been related to the William and Kathleen Hannafin living at number 43 with Margaret. And of those eight or nine, one was a Kathleen. She was living in Slough, though no longer with William. It was a forty-minute journey by car from White City to Slough. As London grew and Londoners had prospered, Slough had prospered at its margins, becoming one of the logical places for people in the west of the city to set up a new home. This Kathleen Hannafin in Slough was an encouraging thought.

The letters I wrote spoke of research into family history. They mentioned a connection with the White City Estate and maybe Ladbroke Grove. I'd be pleased to hear from anyone who'd lived in Mackenzie Close around that time, 'or any of their descendants'. In some cases I explained that I was trying to ascertain what had become of my mother, without mentioning her name; in others, I said nothing of the kind. In others still – to some of the Hannafins, I think – I may have mentioned Margaret's surname, but not that she was my mother. I forget exactly. Each letter carried an apology for writing out of the blue.

The following day was a minor moment of destiny: the certificates I'd ordered would be ready in the Family Records Centre. Marriages (four) and births (four). I felt an urge for the place in any case; a need to repeat the mechanical movement through the registers, quarter by quarter, shelf by shelf. Only it wasn't clear what should be looked for next.

I paid for my certificates and took a chair near the entrance to the search room. In the first marriage certificate, Margaret Walsh married a housepainter at the register office in the Metropolitan Borough of St Pancras in 1956. She was a packer in a printing factory. Her father was a plumber; the groom's father was a railway porter. But she was unlikely to be my Margaret. She was eighteen on the day of the marriage – too young – and living away to the east in Islington.

In the second, Margaret Walsh married an industrial painter at Our Lady of Sorrows in Paddington in 1956. She was a hotel receptionist. Her father was a gang-master and her father-in-law was a train driver in Ireland. The couple lived near Paddington Station in a terrace which has since ceased to exist. She might well have been my Margaret Walsh, but I would have to open a line on the husband's family to find that out.

Next came Margaret Walshe of Hammersmith – a few minutes south of White City – marrying a clerical officer for the Coal Board in 1958 at the Church of the Most Holy Trinity, Brook Green. She was a 'cosmetic consultant'. Both fathers – his a 'licensed victualler', hers a farmer – were dead. She was twenty-five at the time, which, if she were my Margaret, made her a year or two older than I'd imagined. I tried to attach this new possibility to the structure of uncertainties and half-confirmed suspicions that I'd been working on, without the whole edifice pirouetting slowly to the floor. I liked the 'e' on her surname. And the fact that her father was a farmer squared with John Webb's description of the girl he'd met at Harriet and Conrad's. I underlined the address of the groom on the certificate, as though she might still be there, in Westminster, half a century later, advising her loyal, elderly clients about a new moisturiser.

Then came a St Valentine's Day wedding, in high style as I imagined, between Margaret Walsh, spinster, of Baron's Court – not far from White City – and a pie-maker's stoker. The year was

1957. His father was a fisherman, hers was a 'road repairer'. They, too, were married at Holy Trinity in Brook Green. But her age counted against her. A pregnant fourteen-year-old working as a counter assistant in a shop was closer to Dickens or even Lionel Bart than it was to London in the 1950s.

By the time all four brides had been ruled out, I felt irked and exhausted.

If the Family Records Centre allowed you to burrow back into the walled-off parts of your clan warren, it also gave you plenty of scope to invent the bigger thing for yourself in the form of an ethnic past. The mouths of larger tunnels beckoned, even in these certificates. Standing at the edge of a word like 'farmer' and peering over, I could feel the downdraught whispering to me about Irishness. 'Fisherman', 'farmer', 'gang-master', 'Railway Engine Driver (Eire)'. So much for the grandparents. Then the first-generation exiles: housepainter, industrial painter, stoker – all the Margaret Walsh grooms, bar the Coal Board clerk, were caught in the attitudes of a tough immigrant drama.

Later I spent hours envisaging those lives glimpsed in the certificates. Hard lives, some of them. I mapped them on to everything I knew about migrations from Ireland. 'Irishness' was an attractive thing to me, just as I'd once found the idea of a Norse father attractive. Still, I was too guarded and unattached to think that any of this had a bearing on Margaret's boy and the person he'd turned into. But what bearing did it have on Mother One?

The moment had come to examine the birth certificates of possible siblings. In each of them – for John, Carol, Angela and 'Girl' – column five was the main item: 'Name, surname and maiden surname of mother'. It was here that the full name 'Margaret Walsh' might appear in print again (the red volumes, where the births are registered, do not supply the mother's first name).

Angela was born in Hammersmith Hospital. Her mother, though 'formerly Walsh', was called Mary. She'd gone on to marry Angela's father – a Nigerian – and to become Mary Odim.

John, too, was born in Hammersmith Hospital to a mother living in north London who worked as a cashier for a department store, but her name was Bridget. She'd been living – or quartered as a single mother – miles away in Highgate at the time. The certificate had been filled out in a clumsy longhand and under column four, 'Name and surname of father', there was a dash, half an inch long, the tidiest thing on the document.

I looked around the search room, putting off the remaining certificates for a moment or two. The bats swirled in the gallery of a billion names, worrying at the sheer walls of red, green and black.

Carol was born in November 1957 on Harrowdene Road in the district of Willesden, sub-district Wembley. The entry was typed, and under column five, Margaret Walsh was spelled without the 'e'. She was 'an Assistant House Mother, Childrens Home'. Under column seven, she was given as residing on Wembley Park Drive at the time of registration, April 1958. There was nothing about the father.

This, I felt sure, was the one.

I cast a glance at the birth certificate of the Girl. Born Queen Charlotte's Hospital, living in Arundel Gardens, W11. But the mother's name was Julia. The longhand G of 'Girl' was attractively looped in a fine clerical hand. Under column four for the father, there was a one-inch line, done with a ruler. At the right-hand edge of the entry was a longhand diagonal line, left rising to right, and in the same hand the word 'Adopted', above the name of the Superintendent Registrar.

Carol Walsh then. Daughter of Margaret.

An assistant at the enquiries desk knew where you had to go to consult the electoral rolls for Wembley.

I no longer recollect the place. A long ride on the underground, two changes, and somewhere out on the Jubilee Line. A brisk walk and then a public library with a handful of people at microfiche scanners, whirring like pedal sewing-machines.

It seemed so logical. You were a young woman from Ireland, you turned a few heads, but the men were no good to you. Still, you were all right at children: the first had gone for adoption, you were carrying another and when you looked for help midway through your second pregnancy, you happened on a bit of luck – someone in the modest establishment at which you'd made enquiries decided to engage your services as an assistant house mother. You liked the work. You had the second child. You didn't put it out to adoption, and maybe, one way or another, you were able to resume your childcare duties, once the baby was born.

Later, watching researchers at the microfiche screens assembling the vast fabric of the dead and gone, I thought this stab at Margaret's past was too far-fetched. A young girl carrying a second illegitimate child was not going to walk into a job in any mother and baby home. At the time Margaret's second child – my sister, or half-sister, Carol – was born, there were about 180 of these institutions in Britain. They evolved from the mid-eighteenth-century reformatories for penitent prostitutes, whose rehabilitation involved a stringent regime of laundry and prayer. Even by the time of Carol's birth, the guiding notion was still that a mother in need of help was largely to blame for her own misfortunes. It was possible, of course, that the address in Wembley was an establishment of this kind. One of the addresses, that's to say, for in fact there were two. Under the first column of the certificate, 'When and where born', it stated that Margaret had given birth to Carol in a house on Harrowdene Road, also in Wembley.

I ordered up the electoral rolls. Nineteen fifty-six, when Margaret's name had last appeared in Mackenzie Close, seemed a sensible year to start. There was no sign of her on Harrowdene Road, and certainly no evidence to suggest either of the addresses had been a mother and baby home, but it wasn't long before I found Margaret on Wembley Park Drive in 1957, the year of Carol's birth, living in a block of flats.

She held her position in the lists for two years and in 1959 she re-emerged in a partnership – or that was my guess – as Margaret Drew, of Margaret and Robert C. Drew, still in the same building. By 1960 she and her husband had gone, and so had most of the residents in the flats.

The journey back into central London felt slow. The contents of the notebook now included a list of neighbours from Wembley

Park Drive. And there were the Drews themselves.

At my hosts' house, I tapped into the website and stayed up late into the night hunting for any trace of these people, fifty years on.

The following morning I printed off the letters I'd prepared for a dozen or more recipients. I was looking for anyone who remembered Margaret Walsh, later Drew, or knew what might have become of her in the 1960s. And for Drews themselves, I asked if they might be related to the couple on Wembley Park Drive.

I opened an offline file and wrote down what I knew so far about Margaret Walsh:

Margaret Walsh was born in Ireland. She arrived in London not long after the end of the Second World War. She was probably in her mid-teens and almost certainly looking for work. She was friendly with an Irish immigrant couple who lived in Kensal Rise. It was through them that John Webb of Mitcham, near Croydon, encountered Margaret some time in the early 1950s. He found her shy. In the autumn of 1951 she conceived and in 1952 gave birth to a boy named Jeremy, whom she put up for adoption. She kept the baby for eleven days. She was living at the time either on Chesterton Road or in Mackenzie Close with a couple called William and Kathleen Hannafin. She was working in a place known as Chain Stores, apparently in the close, though there is no record, or any sign, of a shop having been there. She became eligible to vote in 1954 and left the White City Estate three years later. By then she may already have found a job as a childcare assistant. In any case, she moved out to Wembley and gave birth to a girl called Carol at the end of 1957. In 1959 or 1960 she married Robert Drew. By 1962 she and Robert were no longer in their apartment on Wembley Park Drive.

That rather left things hanging.

I posted the letters before noon the following day and took a bus to the Family Records Centre.

On the lower deck, seated next to an elderly lady, I began looking over my four birth certificates for Walsh offspring. It took a moment or two to establish beyond doubt that there never was a shop in Mackenzie Close. Columns five and seven of the Girl's birth certificate were what did it. The Girl's mother was described in column five ('Name, surname and maiden name of mother') as 'Julia Walsh, Shop Assistant, Bakers, and Confectioners, of 47 Arundel Gardens, Kensington' and in column seven ('Signature, description and residence of informant') as 'J. Walsh, Mother, 47, Arundel Gardens'.

John's mother, under John's column five, was 'Bridget WALSH Cashier – Departmental Stores, St Helen's Gardens, Kensington', and under column seven she was residing in Highgate. But the existence of a department store in St Helen's Gardens was unlikely. I began rearranging the wording of column five in each certificate: 'Bridget WALSH of St Helen's Gardens, Kensington: Cashier, Departmental Stores'; 'Julia Walsh of 47, Arundel Gardens, Kensington: Shop Assistant, Bakers & Confectioners', etc. And now, retrieving my own birth certificate from the depths of my bag, I jostled the wording of column five – 'Margaret Walsh, Counter Assistant, Chain Stores, of 43, Mackenzie Close, Hammersmith' – to produce 'Margaret Walsh of 43, Mackenzie Close, Hammersmith: Counter Assistant, Chain Stores'.

Not even Ann Pike, my adoption counsellor, had noticed the ambiguity.

The perplexing fact remained that Margaret Walsh, like Bridget Walsh, had cited two residential addresses, but it wasn't a problem that needed an answer now that the mystery of the shop was out of the way.

'Yes, dear, go for it,' said the ancient person in the seat beside me.

I'd been laughing out loud.

'I'm so sorry,' I said.

'No, dear, you enjoy yourself.' She squinted at the sheaf of birth certificates in my lap. 'I'm sure they're an absolute scream.'

The detail that needed attending to in the search room took the form of Edward Stephen Walshe, Margaret's predecessor on the electoral rolls for Mackenzie Close. I supposed he might be a brother. Perhaps if I were to find him marrying, I'd have an idea where he'd gone on to live. Maybe I'd locate his children. Edward S. was less commonplace than Margaret, but it didn't help much. I had to treat the 'e' on Walshe with suspicion, and then discount the 'Stephen', with the result that I was poring over weddings for hundreds of Edward Walshes. In 1950 one of them married a Collins bride in Ealing, but when I looked under C to establish her first name, I found that the only Collins marrying in Ealing in that quarter had taken up with an Edward Marsh. Walsh to Marsh and vice versa was an easy mistake for a clerk to make, especially if the hand in the parish record was hard to read. I became demoralised and lit off, by way of a diversion, to the Hardings, to find Colin and Maureen joined in matrimony. I'd never known the date, but I discovered them in the first quarter of 1951. Colin Aubrey Harding to 'Mathieson/Withcombe'. Mathieson was recognisable: it was Graham's surname, as well as my sister Jill's and my brother Peter's. But the other name was new to me and it wasn't long before I was hunting Maureen Withcombe down. I found no sign of her.

In the evening, I made a list of every living Edward S. Walsh and Walshe from the internet and wrote off a handful of letters, but I held out very little hope of a reply.

It was 10 December. Shopping days to Christmas was no longer the way to look at it. In the pandemonium of internet buying and round-the-clock opening at every Chain Store, where every young Margaret was worked to her wits' end, there were still some fourteen days to go before the frenzy abated, if it ever did. The postal service was a worry. It was congested, perhaps at this very moment setting like refrigerated gravy. My letters would be making their way through a consommé of affection, non-committal and ingratiation, and I wasn't sure how they'd fare. I was anxious, above all, that the letter to John Webb, my hallucinated Father One, might have pitched across the threshold in Surrey and lain there flapping in a mass of junk greetings from high-street businesses.

Jess Hewitt ran a service for adopted people who wished to trace their natural parents and parents wishing to trace the children they'd put up for adoption. I'd had her name and details from a friend, but I'd held off getting in touch until now. I rang Jess cold at her house in the West Country, got the answering machine. She returned the call the same afternoon. It was a tricky conversation. Her professional style was deliberately off-putting. She wanted, quite properly, to dispel any illusions on the part of prospective clients that she might reunite them with their long-lost kin.

'On the other hand,' I said, 'I'm aware of the issues.'

'Yes,' she said, 'but are you aware that your birth-mother's very likely to be dead?'

Yes, I said, I was working on that assumption.

'That what, sorry?' I heard from the other end of the line.

'That's what I . . . assume. That she's dead.'

'Then why are you looking for her?' The question was caring-aggressive, but not improper. Someone like Jess would have to probe and test before she undertook to work for you. I felt impatient with all this scrupulousness.

'It's a fair question,' I said, giving the opposition a little more ground and hoping it might turn to sand. 'I don't really know, but . . . well, I'm aware of what you say.'

'Aware' and 'awareness' were useful words in their own right, decoupled from 'issues'. I jotted down 'aware' on the pad by the phone.

She asked me a couple of fair but intrusive questions about my own life. I replied, I thought, with a lawyer's prudence.

Then: 'Have you talked with your partner?'

Pause.

I'm taking stock of that 'with'.

'Yes, she's also . . . we've been over the issues.'

'Well, you sound like a realistic person,' she said with an air of caution, 'and I think we can try and get something started.'

She outlined the rates she charged, which were reasonable, and asked for faxed details of the lists I'd compiled, Walshes of one kind or another, marriages, births, material from the electoral rolls.

In the afternoon I walked along the south bank of the river and stood with my back to the Oxo Tower, studying the runnels in the mud below, as the tide began to turn. The weather was good.

The next morning I waited in for Jess to call.

'It would help', she said, 'to get Margaret's birth certificate.'

She had a feeling it might be available in Dublin, and she knew how to go about that. And Edward Stephen – he was certainly important. I'd better see who he married, if he did.

That was in hand, I said, sort of. She'd get her contact in Dublin to look him up there, along with Margaret. Did I have enough to be going on with?

Yes, there was stuff to do, I said.

'I think you ought to prepare for a disappointment with the Margaret Murphy in Wembley,' she said briskly.

'Why's that?' I asked, without bothering to correct the surname.

'There are a lot of Margaret Murphys,' she replied. 'And there's nothing, so far, to link your birth mother in Mackenzie Close to the person by the same name in Wembley Park Drive.'

My adoptive mother had said there were sisters, later.

'Was your adoptive mother a reliable person? In terms of information?' Jess asked.

'No, not entirely.'

'I'm not saying it's out of the question. But you shouldn't get too over-invested. Really, that's my advice. Don't go too far down that route at the expense of others.'

After the call, I cleaned up a little in my hosts' kitchen, thinking about words like 'work surface', 'over-invested', 'route'. Then I gave some time of day to 'Murphy'.

There was an avalanche of Christmas mail for my hosts, but nothing from Surrey. Why should there be? Even if he'd received my letter, and written back, how would John Webb's communiqué have stood a chance against all this? I folded the latest cull of greeting cards in a flyer for delivery pizza and placed them on the table in the hall.

X

Laughing Water

I went west for a few days, dragged the short-break cursor across the weekend and set off for London again on the Sunday evening. The journey back would be slow: the itinerary involved a stopover in floodland, where I planned, for a few hours, to lose my mind rather more thoroughly than I had already.

I'd stolen a trowel from some friends near Bristol, a gnarled relic with no handle that was lying in their winter borders, and at the first stop for petrol I bought some cut flowers: this and that, with plenty of yellow freesias. An hour and a half later I was at the roundabout on the A4 where the crowds of CND marchers on their way to Aldermaston used to exasperate Colin. The sensation of blundering around in the dark, in a room one ought to have known well but didn't any more: that was often how it felt coming back here, and the feeling began to quicken as I bore off towards Henley-on-Thames.

In the village, I went right at a little crossroads, up and around on myself and parked by a short lane leading up to the cemetery – not the graveyard by the church, but what we used to think of as the overspill, a raised piece of ground surrounded by trees where, when I was growing up, most of the local burials took place. Colin's father was buried here, so was Mim – and I'd buried Rosemary here, next to them, a few years back. In the old days, like members of a sect that pledged intimate solidarity with the dead, teenage couples used to come here to have sex, lying under the trees at the margins of consecrated ground, as discreetly as the lawful occupants.

The trowel was unnecessary. I'd thought to tend the edges of the plot, but of course it was winter, and the grave was in fair order. Only there was nothing to set the flowers in – I should have thought of that. A few graves away, I spotted a spherical vase. No one would mind, surely. I remembered Maureen jabbing stems into the green, crisp, floral foam at the back of the shop to build up a spray.

Maureen and Colin next. Colin anyhow. But this would take longer.

Station Road seemed to be no distance. I drove down under the railway bridge – forty years ago or more, we'd have had to park the car at this time of year and walk, then wade, to arrive at the footbridge over the Loddon to Rosemary Cottage. Colin was carrying his only boy the last part of the way. He set him down on the steep wooden incline, above the water level, which had already submerged the base of the bridge. The boy held on to the lower part of the wooden rail. The current was quick, but everything was safe, an encompassing whirl of browns and ochres, with scum at the reconfigured edges of the water, far higher now, stretching in languid slicks across entire gardens.

The path up here was marked 'Private'. It was the fifth or sixth such sign, twinned with at-your-peril logos, that I'd passed since turning on to Station Road. The whole place had become like a leper colony – all go away and keep away – adorned with the potato-print devices of the security companies: images of security guards in profile, with peaked caps like American commission-aires. The kinds of warning that tell a burglar he's home and dry. Occasionally, too, doggy devices, in the same activities-corner stencil, not quite Anubis, not exactly Rin Tin Tin, certainly not Maureen's snuffling creatures at risk from the socialists.

It took a passionate sense of what was yours and no one else's to create this bland, homogeneous, mortuary realm, all of a piece and all of a dog. And wasn't it cramped and dark here, where wealthy people clung together pretending they didn't in the moistness of the Thames Valley? In the generous spaces of my childhood, Colin's dream of seclusion had come terribly true.

I paused on the footbridge and looked down at the Loddon, seasonally fast, and again Colin was reeling himself back from the dead, as parents will. He appeared to acquiesce in the monumental, focused compositions that my memory devised for him, as though he were posing before a camera. Something he did well. There were many images, in slow succession, until at length he was standing by a flowerbed in the last of his grandiose gardens, drawing on a cigarette. The wet earth on his hands would have smeared the tumbler of scotch and water, which he'd set on the grass by the border as he resumed his weeding. Behind him an Elysian corridor shone with the various triumphs I remembered at different times of the year: the wrinkled petals of a pinkish-bronze hibiscus; a stand of spiky yellow dahlias like infantile suns; a spread of lolling peonies, downcast with the weight of their magnificence; lofty delphiniums that forgot the order of battle at the last moment, becoming a pale blue rabble army. Then the roses. Unlike his mother, who preferred the old roses, Colin grew modern shrubs, startling hybrids, lavish and pungent, which promised the splendours of decay moments after the buds had begun to open. He attended to them like a manager to a troupe of dancing girls, though most of all he loved his sweet peas, dug in early, the tall stakes sunk a month or so later and the writhing exuberance of colour in mid-June. Work and foresight, and the satisfaction of a moderate investment: quite the opposite of his disastrous interest in fast money. A son might have known that much about his father, but I hadn't seen it at the time.

Wasn't it the same idea of sufficiency – of this much and no more – that had led him to instruct for cremation but then, with typical contempt for the rules, to insist that his ashes be thrown in the river? Scattered is a word he'd have avoided. Ten years ago, I'd come down to this bridge with my aunt Rosemary and the village undertaker, a family friend, who'd brought Colin's remains from the crematorium in Reading – a town Colin disliked almost as much as Slough. The undertaker, a little worried to think we were breaking the law, had handed me the jar and kept an eye open for passers-by. With Rosemary peering over the top of the bridge, I'd emptied the off-white, granular powder in a single squall. 'Over we go,' I thought, and in an icy moment I'd understood from the severity of her look that I'd taken thoroughness a little too far by banging the bottom of the upturned container with my free hand.

Then I was back in a long-gone Sunday, trudging over the same bridge in the London direction, part of our itinerant ménage, carrying whatever we needed to take back to town: dogs – larger breeds in those days – the cat, the clanking bottles of spirits and tonic water. A last glimpse of the dinghy, fast on the other side, then Colin puts me up on his shoulders again and we're rounding the field to the railway. He's slight and wiry and smells like a hearth with the fire kept in overnight. The water, too, has a good smell in the amputated gardens, the lawns recoiling from the floods, and the tree trunks, partly immersed, giving off a dank gist of river, like great wicks steeped in a heavy aromatic.

It was years since we'd lived here. To stand on the bridge was now to commit an act of trespass, and I waited for a successor of Colin's to close on me, gesticulating, possibly shouting. But it was quiet. Not a soul. I crossed the bridge a little furtively and made my way past Rosemary Cottage with the intention of reaching Laughing Water, the only plausible house Mim had built here. There'd been a curving path through trees that led you around for forty or fifty yards and brought you out at a clearing, at which point there were two ways: one to the left, which took you to Laughing Water, the other to the right, through the old wrought-iron gate clotted with brambles in summer, leading to the place she'd called Nirvana, where the houseboat had been dragged up on to dry land.

A few yards from the footbridge, the path through the trees was blocked by a new wooden barrier.

It was turning cold. I retraced my steps and sat in the car. There was plenty to consider here, including the fact that two of the houses associated with our family had gone up in flames. Thinking that over would need a moment or two – and another couple of minutes' driving.

The footbridge across the Loddon was not the only way to Laughing Water and Nirvana. For another hundred yards, the road from the station ran parallel with the river and bent around to span it with an angular concrete bridge. Five or six hundred yards beyond that, you were by the Thames.

As I took the car over the concrete bridge, I resisted the temptation to look back downstream in the direction of Laughing Water. Where the track ended, the way to the site of the old houseboat was barred by another large gate with an intercom device. I got out and peered through the trees at the shape of a familiar building a little way from where the houseboat had been.

In the early 1960s Colin had set the tone of our domain for years to come, with a decisive blow against the easygoing, sentimental ways of his mother. Having persuaded her to give him the property on which the houseboat stood, he had insisted, despite her objections, on building a cedar-wood bungalow. Cedar was in vogue just then, and it was cheap. When he announced that he meant to demolish the houseboat, she was so offended that it was towed, at some expense, about fifty yards from the bungalow – the building I could now see through the trees – and left to decay for a year or two in a handsome profusion of weeds and elder, like a customs post reclaimed by jungle. She wouldn't hear of it being destroyed.

One Saturday, when the weather was dry, Colin contrived a fire in the remains of the marooned edifice. The fire brigade had found it difficult to reach the place. The concrete bridge could not take heavy vehicles and the only other access was a roundabout way which added half an hour to the journey. My own devoted Mim, the relative I'd seized on at an early age and confiscated from Colin, was far quicker on to the scene. In her patchwork, theatrical clothes, she took up a position at a safe distance from the blaze and held it like an alabaster statue, one gnarled hand on her shooting stick, the other clutching a handkerchief which she was incapable of raising to her eyes.

The truth about the fire – the first fire – emerged that same evening, in the course of a conversation between Colin and Maureen. I promised to say nothing to Colin's parents or Rosemary. If I'd been serenely puzzled about our secrecy on the matter of my adoption, I could see obvious reasons, in this case, for keeping very quiet. But perhaps, too, I began to have reservations about the way Colin and Maureen carried on.

*

Press the buzzer by the gate, maybe, and talk on the intercom to the new owners of Laughing Water? When I raised myself up near the gatepost, I could see that the ditch forming a natural boundary between the site of the houseboat and the grounds of Laughing Water was now lined with some sort of fence. I'd only to straddle the gate and walk a few yards to get a good view of the bungalow, but I hadn't the heart for it. 'Nirvana'. A state of enlightenment, a state of 'no craving'. Or simply a state of being Maureen, fully topped up, fast asleep on the floor by the sofa after Sunday lunch: no craving there. None for me, either – now I'd made my way to the house, I found I'd no more desire to look at it than I'd had to cast an eye over Mim's old place.

I got back into the car and prepared to head for London, but couldn't raise the will to start the engine.

Was it surprising, I thought now as the first drops of rain fell on the windscreen, that when Colin's mother died, she left Laughing Water to Rosemary? Colin did not contest the decision in court, but his threats to do so were part of the infernal fuss he made so as to bully Rosemary around to his way of thinking – for Colin, thinking was mostly a preamble to getting. He was so intractable, so deeply disagreeable, that within a few years she let him have the house and the land it stood on for £9,000. Any 'family' feelings he may have had about the place were thereby indulged at a stroke. But such feelings, with Colin, had been convertible all along: in his eyes, this was a riverside property, sure to increase in value, much like the bungalow he was already planning to sell. He kept his mother's house standing for a time. Then, mysteriously, this last authentic evidence of her affection for a misty quadrangle of land, ten or fifteen acres in all, set between two rivers and got between two wars for next to nothing, burned to the ground.

Colin had always been eager to do away with the old world of his parents. And now, for a second time, one could only assume, he had disposed of the remains by means of an immense pyre.

At Laughing Water, he continued to develop the new style for our odd corner of the Home Counties by commissioning a luxurious affair in white shingle, further back from the river than the old

139

house. Around the property, the building contractors dug and cut and shifted earth and laid the new foundations. When it was done, everything that hadn't burned or disappeared altogether stood stranded in a seamless inundation of grass. The poplars towered over it all like the furled and isolated emblems of a time that no longer existed. The new era had the blandness and vulgarity of a golf course, and the building at the centre of this sudden transformation was unmistakably a version of the club house. Only the brick tree remained.

It was another form of deluge – not a seasonal thing, overrunning the place with water for a fortnight, but a definitive submersion of part of our lives. It sealed off our domain finally and utterly from what I thought of as reality and turned it into a minor principality. From then on, I'd kept away from it as much as possible without appearing impolite. Colin and Maureen had a few years' use of the property and then Colin sold it for a little more than thirty times what he'd paid Rosemary. Within another few years, there were minor principalities springing up all around, many of them identical to the untrained eye.

Once more, I got out of the car and this time prepared, in earnest, to say some sort of farewell.

Standing in the wet, I had the curious sensation of being about to lift Colin bodily. Not Colin the off-white sugar that I'd poured over the footbridge from the word which escapes me – casket? urn? – but a heavy emanation, as though on contact with the water the powder had set like a packet dessert, an Angel Delight, and shown up now as a kind of person, a kind of father, someone to carry. As a child gets older he should lead his parents back into the world, I told myself, take charge of things, set the disagreements aside – the merits of General Pinochet, all that – vow to protect their pets from the socialists, if necessary. (A drag on the muscles like the weight of contrition; and Colin getting heavier in my arms.)

It's not as if we're a race apart, I seemed to be telling him, as I walked slowly from the car. I heard myself explaining that I had a lawn now, and kept it mowed; there was even a dog. I had money and ease and all the things he'd wanted for himself and for his son. Then I was saying I planned to take him down to the river and put him in again, but properly this time, with more sense of occasion, because he liked the river. We both like the river.

He nods and smiles as he did when he was very ill, at the end of his life. We cross the tall grass in front of the bungalow.

That's odd, I think to myself, this is spring grass.

Summer grass, he says, and the dead weight seems to lift from my arms a little. I look down at him. He's wearing his gardening clothes. Collarless shirt, worsted trousers held up at the waist by a tie, a muddy pair of brogues. Our dinghy is moored by the broken cement steps that served as a landing stage. A lick of paint's in order, I notice.

What now? Do I lower you into the dinghy and set fire to it?

You mean like a Viking funeral?

Yes, I say, something Scandinavian and paradoxical – you in flames on the water, like Balder the Beautiful.

No. Just put me down on my feet, if you would.

He's on the steps, lighting a cigarette. He shakes his trousers out slightly, kneels, takes the dinghy by the prow and coaxes it through the grey water, broadside to the landing stage.

It's Saturday, he says.

I correct him: I think you'll find it's Sunday.

Saturday, he says again. A Saturday in June.

He slides the sculls into the rowlocks while I keep hold of the painter.

I'm going down to the village, he says, to do the shopping. Would you care to join me?

I think I'll stay, I say. There's stuff to do.

He gives a flick of the wrist on one scull, the boat turns slowly about. I lob the painter into the boat.

Just as you like, he says.

As he clears the small island opposite the bank and enters the open water ahead, he's leaning into the stroke. A few seconds later and he's caught the current.

The boat moves swiftly round the first bend and out of sight.

*

Best cut across to the M40 at Burchett's Green, I thought, as I got back in the car. Come in to London on the Westway, past the White City, past Margaret's, I mean. Down off the Marylebone Flyover.

But what of Maureen? I should have done the honours back there.

I tried to track the question in the rear-view mirror. Not the time, I answered, not the place, for a proper leave-taking. That would have to be postponed till I'd found out who she actually was. Even her real name. How many mothers was I looking for?

At Greenford there was congestion and I nudged the hire car along, flipping the preset buttons on the radio. It was good to be drawn back into the city, slowly, as part of a vast Sunday night regurgitation from the ever-extending suburbs.

I was thoroughly expecting word from John Webb to be waiting in Camden. Obviously, I'd be skipping the first couple of lines. My eye would skim for the name 'Margaret' and the word 'father', prefaced perhaps by 'your', at which point I'd backtrack for a significant 'not'.

John would explain how he'd run into Margaret several times more at Harriet and Conrad's place in Kensal Rise and yes, they'd begun to get along. A decade abridged in a single sentence here, a paragraph of detail there. He'd end with the suggestion that he and I meet up and pay a visit to the cemetery where Margaret was buried.

The trouble was that after leaving the hire car in Euston and walking through a cold, beautiful Sunday night in north London, I arrived at the house in Camden to find no such letter in the pile of unopened mail.

In the morning, I rang my brother Peter. He called me 'old boy', as Colin used to, and I liked that.

'Our mother . . .' I began, and he cut me off with a laugh.

'God, please, not our mother.'

I told him what I was up to.

'Where was she from?' I asked. 'I mean originally.'

'Maureen? She was from Streatham.'

'Not Mitcham, Surrey.'

'Well, yes, Mitcham,' he said. He sounded pressed for time. 'Didn't I give you a copy of her birth certificate?'

'Oh Lord. When was that?'

'After the cremation, at the send-off,' he said. 'D'you remember, in that bag of bits and pieces I gave you that belonged to her. I bet you've never looked at them.'

Peter was a good judge of character.

'Well, you look them over when you're home,' he said, 'but if you can't find them, let me know and I'll get you what I call a xerox, or I'll fax the damn thing. How's the family?'

'Family's good,' I said.

I called home straight away, got the comforting foreign ringing tone, but just before the third ring I hung up. If I didn't know what had become of the striped bag full of stuff that belonged to Maureen, why should anyone else?

XI

Relations

She gave her name as Jean and the first thing she asked was whether I'd written to a Philip Drew about Margaret. I had, I said, in a state of serious unreadiness – I'd expected to take a call about a delivery for my hosts. It was cold and I began to shiver.

Her voice was hesitant, but it hadn't the tentative phone manner of the English buffoon, which I was now managing rather well. Ah yes, I said, I'd kind of had it in mind, or I was possibly thinking, and hadn't intended . . . what . . . that's right, to tread on any toes, but I wasn't suggesting and I was sorry if. Up against this barrage of equivocation, the voice at the other end began to falter in its turn.

I started again. I'd written because I thought there might be a connection with Margaret. And perhaps with a daughter called Carol. Well, said the voice, there was a daughter called Carol, but she – Jean – had been born to Margaret Walsh even earlier, in 1945. The family history was so tangled that her father had handed my letter over to her: it upset him to go into it. But yes, she imagined there might be some sort of link between us.

'We'd have to trace Margaret back a bit,' she said. Where was I born? No, there was no connection with Hammersmith that she knew of. I gave her the two addresses on my birth certificate. No, Jean said, there was no connection.

She asked: 'What year was that again?'

I told her 1952. She was with her mother then, and they were nowhere near Ladbroke Grove or the White City Estate.

'It doesn't sound as though it's the same Margaret Walsh.'

'No, it doesn't,' I agreed, feeling the room pitch slightly.

'Were there a lot?' she asked. 'A lot of Margaret Walshes? I've never looked into that sort of thing.'

'Hundreds.'

'Well, that would explain it. Our own connections were East-bourne, Park Royal and Wembley. There's Irish blood in the family. I suppose your Margaret Walsh was Irish?'

'I'm not sure,' I said, 'but it's likely, isn't it?'

'With a name like that? Almost certain to be.'

I thought: Murphy.

She asked if I had blue eyes. Bluish, I said. And hers? Yes, blue. She asked how I was built. Gangly, I said – and her?

'We're none of us gangly,' she said. 'The tallest the men get is five feet ten and they're quite solid.'

I took us back to White City for the last time – if there was no link there, then there was no link at all.

There was no link.

I remember very little of what we said after that. I don't think I asked anything about Carol. But a tremendous sadness hollowed out her voice as she explained a couple of family complications. And then she confessed she was disappointed: she'd been so happy when her father gave her the letter. She'd thought she'd come by a brother.

She gave me her phone number, in case anything stood the story on its head. We were wishing each other luck as the front door bell rang. On my way through the hall it rang again. I opened the door to find two delivery men standing either end of a large Christmas tree.

Jess Hewitt had been right to caution against a jump from White City to Wembley. It was a leap of the imagination only. But I could hardly bear to watch the tide roll back, leaving Margaret stranded in the White City, exactly where she was half a century ago.

So it was the tube to Shepherds Bush – the Central Line – then the Uxbridge Road, but this time I cut west off Bloemfontein Road towards the Wormholt Estate and rang a bell on Bryony Road. Violet Palfrey hadn't answered my letter, but I'd rung and she'd asked me over, and now she showed me in. She was a kind, tired-looking woman in her late sixties or early seventies, a bit suspicious at first. She sat me in the kitchen. The TV was on in the room

145

next door and I could see the head and legs of a large figure in an armchair.

They'd lived in Mackenzie Close in the 1950s. She'd been with her parents in number 40, on the ground floor. There was a bomb shelter, she remembered, and a wash-house next door, with a mangle. But she couldn't think of any Hannafins or Walshes. We talked about the other neighbours, a family called the Wests and some McCarthys. Violet had lost touch with most of them. It was so long ago, she said.

Somebody was smoking. I don't remember if it was Violet or the man in front of the TV. I remember the smell of tobacco. She made coffee. She was wearing a dark blue polo-neck top in a stretch fabric, and a pair of slacks. I couldn't read her well, and I couldn't read the house. I'd lost the ability to size up people and places on a first encounter – and I'd begun falling aimlessly, or gently rotating in zero gravity, with the familiar markers of class and social identity turning gently around me like luminous debris in the aftermath of a space-probe disaster.

Then I was touching down. And I could feel the weary generosity of the household, which I took to be part of the person Violet Palfrey was.

She said it had been a proper community.

'Community?' I said.

'White City. You know what I mean?'

I thought I might.

'The thing was, everyone minded their own business, otherwise I'd know more than I do about number 43. But if anyone had a problem, my mother and father sort of rallied round. Everyone rallied round.'

I wondered was it still like that? Violet didn't think so. And they'd moved out here, bought this place a stone's throw from the old estate, where they'd been in several different flats over the years, in order to get away from the downhill slide.

'Still,' said Violet, 'it's no better here.'

She thought it was lawless and noisy and loutish and she had the house on the market now. I said it seemed so pleasant and she

146

laughed. In a way I was right, she said, one shouldn't complain.

'Half a century is a long time,' I said, getting back to the point, and thought to myself that if I'd tried to establish anything about Margaret twenty, thirty years back, when memories would have been fresher and more people would have been around, I'd have run the risk of her being alive. It was frustrating to have done it this way, but now only one of us could come as a shock to the other.

Although you know, Violet said abruptly, one of the West boys from Mackenzie Close was working as an estate agent now. He might have an idea what had become of the people at number 43. She'd talk to Ron.

Ron was a relative, I forget what, maybe Violet's uncle or older brother. Ron had a line to everyone.

I told Violet about Margaret's being my mother and she rang Ron straight away, but there was no reply. She said he must be on the golf course.

The house was small and orderly and very calm, even with the TV squirting mid-afternoon babble through the whole of the downstairs. We agreed to speak on the phone a bit later. Ron was my man, if anyone was, and I wasn't to worry, she'd be in touch.

On Bloemfontein Road I stopped and stared across at the row of shops flanking the White City Estate. Then I took off for the Uxbridge Road, thinking I wouldn't be back here for a time. I was running out of notions.

Towards the end of the week there were two letters. The first was from a well-disposed lady – a Burton – who had the same given name as the Burton I'd found in the old electoral rolls for Chesterton Road. But she wasn't the same person, and was surprised – most people are – to hear that there was another person with her name. She was in north-west London. She'd never lived in Chesterton Road, 'though we sometimes took our dog to a tiny park in St Quintin Avenue near by'. She wrote: 'I can well understand the need for knowledge of your mother, as I feel similar about my paternal grandparents, and their relation to Richard Burton (the Scholar and Explorer).'

The second was from an Edward S. Walsh in Sheffield and it had come promptly, through the drifts of Christmas mail. Which led me to realise that the people who intended to reply to the faintly intrusive post I'd sent would have done so immediately or not at all. They might have said to themselves that they'd sit on the letter and think things over, but in the end, the reflection would only prolong the sitting, and if I hadn't heard from them already, I shouldn't expect to.

Two replies – no, three, counting Jean's phone call – from seventy letters or so was fair, I thought, but how many people had greeted my request for information as the work of a charlatan or a madman?

'I don't think I'm your man,' Eddie Walsh wrote. 'My middle name is Stanley.' He was born in London – King's Cross – and he'd joined the Navy in 1960. 'I never knew my father, who was an American GI.' He couldn't come up with a White City affiliation or an Edward Stephen. 'In a way I'm sorry,' he finished off, very much like Jean, 'I would have liked a brother.'

I folded his letter and kept it in the pocket of my jacket for the rest of my stay in London, along with the letter from Diana Burton, whose distant forebear had entered Mecca disguised as a Pathan pilgrim.

Three out of seventy, I thought again, and now it seemed a lame response. Violet Palfrey hadn't been offended when I rang. So it was a good idea to follow up a letter with a phone call.

I stood at the window in my hosts' kitchen watching the weather pretend to lift.

John Webb.

The rapid hold that Christmas was taking on the city, spreading across it by the hour, was exciting and so I settled instead on Christmas shopping. However tawdry and craven the thing had become, Christmas remained the stuff of childhood promise. I set out decisively, with a view to some novelties for my children's stockings. I emerged after two hours with a shirt I couldn't resist and five CDs – recordings I hadn't heard in years. When I got back, there was a message from Ron Palfrey. I rang him. He was upbeat, magnificent even.

'We're going to find that mother of yours,' he said, 'if I have to turn out the whole of the old White City Estate. I mean, it's a big thing, this. A man wants to know about his mother, it's common sense.'

The voice reminded me of Stanley Holloway. It was bluff and reassuring.

I said I didn't imagine Margaret was alive, but at least I'd like to know what had happened to her.

Ron had made a call to one of the Wests of Mackenzie Close. And there was someone else called Joanie, who'd been on the estate in 1954. She was sure to know of a Walsh, was it? That's a tough one, I thought of saying, because it just might be a Murphy.

Anyway, he'd left a message with Joanie. Yes, and a couple by the name of Edwards – 'the fellow, you know, the Edwards fellow, I used to court his sister' – they'd almost certainly be able to help.

It was all a bit like the Twilight Barking in *One Hundred and One Dalmatians*, when the dogs howl out the news of a sinister disappearance, which is transmitted from hilltop to valley. Only this time, it wasn't a parent putting out the call, but an ageing puppy who'd found a well-placed senior dog to do it for him.

The quietness of the Hannafins was beginning to unnerve me. Not a single letter back. I spoke to a Jeremy Hannafin. Yes, he'd had the letter, he said patiently, but no, he couldn't help me. I rang a Sarah Hannafin, who took me for a lunatic caller with something intelligent and awful in mind. I thought about Kathleen, dug deep into Slough, refusing to respond. Her phone number hadn't shown up on my internet search. Perhaps she was ex-directory. Why? And when would Ron Palfrey come up with a connection? And how had I managed to pursue the wrong Margaret Walsh in Wembley? Why had that diversion seemed so promising? The story of the missing siblings, so casually told by Maureen, master of the big, blurry picture, must have influenced my thinking. Every hint she'd ever thrown me confirmed her gift for nonsense and my own susceptibility. But Maureen wasn't the root of it: there was something intrinsically maddening about this business of looking. A few meagre facts, hard won, tended to grow into wild assumptions, while a straightforward lead would quickly curve away from a possible destination and dance off into an arc of illusion.

The story of Margaret Walsh would need revising. I opened up the computer file for the first time in a while. Since then, it had become plain that the Chain Stores was not in Mackenzie Close, and horribly plain that I'd been following the wrong Margaret in Wembley. The entry shrank accordingly:

Margaret Walsh was born in Ireland. She arrived in London not long after the end of the Second World War. She was probably in her mid-teens and almost certainly looking for work. She was friendly with an Irish immigrant couple who lived in Kensal Rise. It was through them that John Webb of Mitcham, near Croydon, encountered Margaret some time in the early 1950s. He found her shy. In the autumn of 1951 she conceived and in 1952 she gave birth to a boy named Jeremy, whom she put up for adoption. She kept the child for eleven days. She was living then or a little later in Mackenzie Close with a couple called William and Kathleen Hannafin. She was working in a place described as a Chain Stores: it was probably Woolworth's. She became eligible to vote in 1954 and left Mackenzie Close a few years afterwards.

I read it over and closed the file. I rang directory enquiries. Kathleen Hannafin didn't have an ex-directory number. She didn't have a phone number at all.

That would be all right, John had said. Should he fetch me from Morden station in his black cab?

No, I'd get the 93 down to the big pub just beyond his house – 'or the 81,' he put in helpfully – and double back from there. I knew my way now.

'I suppose that's right,' he'd said.

I mentioned nothing about the letter, nothing about Margaret. Just that it'd be good to meet before I headed home.

The weather was fine. Cold and clear in parts of the south-east. An agreeable breeze had rid the city of its drear look. The suburbs felt lively, up for anything, the bus from Morden underground station was full. As it passed John Webb's house on the way to the stop a few hundred yards beyond, I saw there'd been some changes. He'd warned me on the phone that I couldn't miss the decorations, even though they wouldn't be lit at this time of day. On the flat balcony at the front, above the generous bay, there was a plastic figure of Santa Claus, several feet high, profiled in an enormous sled with a complement of reindeer.

'We do this every Christmas,' he said, as he showed me in.

'Yes,' said his wife, 'and this year it's done for his back as well.'

'It gets harder,' he said. 'I expect I should have hung on. A friend was coming by to give us a hand, but I thought I'd put it up there, you know, thought I'd probably manage it.'

Gingerly, he took a seat on the sofa. I asked if he was in pain. Vicky Webb got up with things to do. I was sat in the armchair, in the bay.

We turned around and about for a time, then I asked him if he'd got my letter. He had. I asked had he been able to think about it?

'Oh, I've thought about it,' he said. 'Of course, I should tell you right away I'm not your father.'

I gave him a breezy, apologetic laugh, taking the imaginary weight of the enormous Father Christmas display on the flat section of roof above my head. No doubt I managed something clever or charming. I wanted him to feel at ease – that was my only plan now that Morden, too, had suddenly become a dead end.

'It was a long shot,' he said.

'A long shot and the last shot,' I replied.

'I'd have been perfectly happy to be your father. But I can't oblige.'

'I'd have made a passable son,' I replied. 'But as it turns out, I can't oblige either.'

He looked a little older than I remembered. I scanned the laughter lines around the eyes as though I were running my fingers over a set of scars. Then I remembered he was in pain.

What did he make of Maureen saying my natural father was a waiter in the Merchant Navy?

'I think she made it up,' he said without hesitation. 'She felt she'd have to tell you some story or other, she thought about it, and when she let her mind go along a bit, she hit on what I'd been up to. It was instinct, you see – I'll take that bit from John's life and I'll put it into the pot. Maureen could do that sort of thing. And that's how your father came to be a waiter in the Merchant Navy.'

That seemed right. Maureen's fib was the kind of thing I'd have tried in my time. But then again, John had answered with such assurance that I began to suspect it might be the kind of fib he'd have tried too. Father and son, for a moment there. Finally, I ascribed his decisive view of it to the simple fact that he'd had time to think it over. I wondered about the Scandinavian thing. He had no suggestions.

What about Margaret? Was there anything more he'd remembered? He said it was a long time ago.

'I suppose I'm sitting right under your Father Christmas, and the sleigh and the reindeer?'

'The roof's very solid,' he said. 'And the decorations – they look substantial, but they're plastic. Doesn't weigh a lot. D'you know, I don't even recall the colour of your Margaret's hair.'

I thought of the girlfriend on the kibbutz.

He began again on the story of Maureen's first husband arranging for his flight from Colombo when his father was dying. And then he ducked back a decade, to the early part of the war, when Graham had taken him on at the big house in Caterham. He used to cycle in, he said, and one day he'd been blown off his bike by a bomb blast. He'd been a bit bruised, and the bike chain was done for. And so when he travelled to Caterham after that, he used to take a spare one. For a few seconds, I was back in my infantile train-yard, where I'd marshalled *Oliver!* and *Pygmalion*, only now I was coupling up two unrelated incidents by fitting the blinding moment in the Bren carrier in Palestine behind the bomb in Surrey, clicking and clacking them this way and that. Through the privacy of this distraction, I still saw the man very clearly, with his bad back and his Christmas decorations, me under them, him on the sofa, well clear in the event of a disaster. Did I glimpse my children? The middle boy. But again, wasn't that his mother's looks?

'Are there any presents?' I asked.

'Presents?'

'In the sleigh, you know – up there.' I raised my eyes to the ceiling.

'If I'd known you were coming . . .'

In this, the season of wish-making, I wished most of all that I'd stuck my letter to John, my fantastic Father Christmas, up the chimney of some empty ruin miles from civilisation.

He rose from his seat with a bit of difficulty. In a room overlooking the garden at the back, we went through a few photos I hadn't seen on my first visit – mostly the old cars he'd kept, though there was another picture of his daughter. I forced myself not to look for a likeness to anyone. Outside it was getting dark; time to take people at their word.

When Vicky came back, we talked about the trouble with Britain. It was a healthy, careless, energetic, venal place, I protested.

She agreed. But the British – the native British – didn't want to work any more.

I saw Margaret coming down a gangway, off a boat. Liverpool, surely. Or was it Fishguard?

John steered the cab in, opposite the underground entrance, and we shook hands. Happy Christmas. He left the door to his life ajar. I could get in touch any time. I was thinking about his bad back. How he'd be having to wrest his upper body round to check the traffic, before he pulled out and turned for home.

For years I'd imagined adoption in terms of a fable of blood and water, and imagined it relentlessly to my advantage. Now a wish to be done with water as an image of civility and good sense was gathering pace. But the story of not belonging had so many uses. You couldn't look at a person, as most people might look at their mother or father, and say with any assurance: yes, I know how I came by this habit or that tendency. And without the workings of attribution, it was as though you were answerable to nobody.

In some sense this marvellous exemption had been grasped too avidly and 'nobody', it struck me now, had become a version of myself. Nobody was an easy description under which to abscond. All you had to do was reaffirm the fact that you'd never quite been what anyone had in mind. In my own eyes this had given me a secret authority, and confirmed me in the opinion that mine was the only impartial way of understanding things: most other people were condemned to peer at the world across the obscurity of the breeding-hutch. A shrewd, elusive nobody saw things in their proper light. I'd learned, too, to give 'nobody' the benefit of the doubt – systematically, on every possible occasion. It was an ingenious form of licence, hard to forgo.

Pride was at stake, I suppose, in my taking the loss of John Webb as hard as I did. I'd got it superbly wrong. So much for the fluent intuitions of the boy raised by water. But it probably went deeper. Whatever the gist of my fable, I'd wanted to be rescued from the river again, out of the blue, by a father of sorts. I'd wanted to dry off, perhaps conclusively.

The Hannafins. I'd been unduly optimistic about them, too. Kathleen, in any case. If they meant to keep to themselves, that was their affair. To their credit, they'd done so with flawless discipline, like synchronised swimmers performing 'the empty pool' – barely a ripple on the surface, not a limb in prospect. They'd shown a sort of mute solidarity and they were intelligent. Kathleen especially was good at sorry I'm not here, a devious game at which I thought I was unbeatable. I picked up the phone and called directory enquiries again. No, she wasn't a subscriber.

Two more days in London. I'd begun to pack, in preparation for my return home. Whatever had failed to come good, there was always Christmas. After another foray to the shops to buy presents for my children, I emerged from a department store on Oxford Street wearing a new watch strap and carrying a pair of curtains for our guest-room at home.

There was little to be done here now. A couple of lines of inquiry remained open. There was Jess, hunting through the Dublin registers on my behalf: with the information I'd sent her, she'd be on to Walshes rather than Murphys by now. And there was Ron Palfrey. The Twilight Barking could still come good. Ron Palfrey was the right stuff and well connected, if he said so himself.

I woke early. The dawn light was on the roofs. An hour later the sun was up, followed shortly by my hosts, in good spirits. They were going to decorate the Christmas tree. There was a party planned for the evening. It would be full of people who knew exactly who they were and what they were about, and I found myself looking forward to it.

But it must be her.

A nagging conviction that the Kathleen Hannafin lying low in Slough was crucial.

I walked through the sunshine, joined the first turnout of morning shoppers at the bus stop on Camden Road and by ten-thirty I was standing among the black registers in the search room of the Family Records Centre. A William Hannafin who'd died in Slough would be proof enough that the Kathleen who'd kept so skilfully out of everyone's way was the survivor of the couple Margaret Walsh had shared a flat with in Mackenzie Close. Before long, I had my hands on a sombre black ledger, with its promise of a piece in the middle of a jigsaw – full of missing bits in any case – of which I'd failed to assemble a single corner.

There was only one other researcher on this shadowy terrace: a shambling man in his mid-seventies, with a magnifying glass and long, flaxen hair. As soon as he bent over an entry in one of the registers, the hair, which had been drawn to the front of the head to form a pelmet, swooned on to the lists of dead. Every so often he threw it back or held it to one side, like a terrible bride bearing her withered train. There was an undignified smell of urine and Parmesan cheese about and around him. He moved with an unearthly speed along the shelves. I was about six years ahead of him and meant, if I could, to keep it that way.

I began on the Hannafin dead, with four spellings of the surname, at 1965. There weren't many to be had: fourteen of any interest by the time I'd covered a decade, including a William John Hanifan – a fifth variant – in Westminster in 1972. The men, I noticed – even in my haste to keep ahead of my grim contender – didn't live long. There were a few who'd lived into their eighties, it was true, but most of these people – immigrant labourers or their children – had been born during or after the First World War, and would have been in their late fifties or early sixties at the time of their deaths.

The reeking pallbearer was closing on me as I logged the name of Terence Hannafin, born 'about 1903', died 1978 in Derby. Not quite a generation on and they'd begun to live longer. Now came a William Hannafin, dead in 1988 at the age of sixty-four, and a William Hanifan, dead at the age of fifty-seven, which wasn't so old. But neither of these Williams died in the right place.

The William Hannafin I was looking for appeared in 1993. His death was recorded in Slough. He was in his early seventies. I shut the last of the black volumes, shrugged the stiffness out of my shoulders and left the deaths section.

XII

Voices

By late afternoon, when I got back to the house, preparations were under way for the party. The phone rang. It was Violet Palfrey.

'I was talking to Ron,' she said.

Apparently he'd been in touch with a neighbour from the old days who remembered a big lady at number 43 scrubbing the stairs and taking in a lot of children.

'He thinks she looked after them as a babysitter, or perhaps she was a foster mother. No one seems to remember.'

We mulled over her information for about a minute and a half.

Vi's anxious face, the kitchen on Bryony Road.

'Is Ron about?' I asked. 'It might be worth me giving him a call.'

'He's off out tonight,' Vi said. 'Best try him tomorrow, after dinner.'

It was good of her to ring.

No, it was no trouble. She'd keep in touch.

I'd written to Kathleen Hannafin, I'd tried to find her phone number and failed, and now I had her up on the internet search. When I shuffled about a bit, it was prepared to supply a list of her neighbours. I noted down the names and went into a different menu to see if it would offer their phone numbers. I was thinking of Violet's description of a 'big lady' and wondering whose children they'd been crawling across the Hannafins' floor, or burbling on the balcony outside the flat in summer, with a view over the incinerator.

Four neighbours in all, but I couldn't draw a single phone number. Did they have something against telephones in Kathleen's corner of Slough?

I dragged a call-taker at directory enquiries through four names and addresses. He failed to produce a number for any. I waited a few minutes and rang again. The new voice at the end of the line was a bit more promising, and when she began to doubt my intentions, I told her it was a problem with an elderly relative who hadn't answered the phone: the time had come to contact a neighbour.

I got a line to a Mrs Edith Moore. I was sorry, of course, but was I right in thinking she might be a neighbour of Kathleen Hannafin?

'Well, I might,' she said. 'That's right.'

She sounded like an elderly quiz-show hostess. I was trying to get in touch with Kathleen. I lived abroad. I wasn't sure, but I thought my connection with Kathleen went back fifty years, to the old days on the White City Estate. Well, with a friend of Kathleen's actually, who lived with her at the time.

'But Kathleen passed away,' said Mrs Moore. 'She passed away in the summer.'

Deceased.

I went rummaging in all my heartless places for a word of condolence, but it didn't look promising. And then, like a flash: 'I'd no idea.'

'Nor had we,' said Mrs Moore. 'It was that sudden.'

'I'm so sorry.'

'Nor had we,' she repeated. 'Mind you, she hadn't been well.'

'Well, quite,' I said.

'Not that we're any of us getting any younger.'

'You mean in Slough?' I asked unaccountably.

'Well, I suppose that's it,' Mrs Moore said.

Kathleen had died in July and the line had been disconnected. Mrs Moore thought the flat, across the way from hers, was still unoccupied. So another crucial link had been severed, by a drastic yet reliable process whose results I'd been admiring in the black registers earlier that day. Maybe there was a way to contact some of Kathleen's relatives?

'Well, it depends who,' said Mrs Moore, suddenly a little carefree. 'There's so many of them. Dozens, actually.'

She began on a list of names, first names only, of which I jotted down a couple. The name Margaret came up, but it had come up so often now that I simply scrawled it somewhere between 'Mary' and 'Gerald'.

'Big Irish family,' she said.

She was careful not to divulge any details; it wouldn't be right to give out phone numbers.

'But if you leave your own,' she said amiably, 'and tell me your name again, I'll be seeing some of them next Tuesday . . .'

Today was Thursday. I was leaving early on Saturday. I gave her my name. I gave her my number abroad, said again that the connection went back many years, and took the form of a young woman sharing with the Hannafins in Mackenzie Close during the 1950s: Mrs Moore seemed to get all that.

'So if I'm seeing them Tuesday, there'll probably be someone in touch on Wednesday – next Wednesday,' she said.

'That's Christmas Eve,' I said.

'Yes,' she said, 'I'd see them then normally.'

'Yes, but I mean they won't want to ring on Christmas Day, will they?'

'That's true,' she said. 'More like the Friday.'

'Perhaps I could give you a call on Friday anyhow – I mean, if nobody from the family's been in touch?'

'I can't see any harm in that. Only I'll be at my daughter's. Or will I?'

She couldn't seem to remember.

The dining-room table had been set back against a wall. I began opening the white wine, replacing the corks part way and boring the bottles into a sink full of ice in the kitchen. I went to the fridge, poured a large vodka, put some black pepper in it and drank it down. I felt defeated – but now it was party time. I was starting on the reds when the phone rang.

'Yes, I'm . . .'

But before I could confirm it, the voice on the other end of the line said, 'I gather you're taking an interest in my family.'

I said maybe, or I wasn't sure – it sort of depended on who the caller was.

The voice was that of a youngish woman, I guessed, London, or somewhere within range of the city, but there was a lot of bustle round me now, with the guests due to arrive, and I asked her to hold while I went to another phone.

She was testing. She told me she'd just heard from Edie Moore, Kathleen's neighbour. I said yes, I'd spoken to Mrs Moore and left a number with her, but I hadn't expected to hear from anyone until after Christmas. Sure, sure, she said, but why did I want to know about the White City Estate? I said I thought I had a connection with someone who'd shared a flat with Kathleen.

'Kathleen and William,' she said. 'When would that have been?'

'In the early 1950s,' I said, 'half a century . . .'

'And who was the person you think you were connected with?'

I told her Margaret Walsh.

'And what kind of connection d'you think you had with her?'

'I think I might be a relation – related to the Walshes.'

'Yes, but to Margaret in particular?'

'I think it's possible, but I don't know for sure.'

'Well, why don't you try to explain?' she said. 'By the way, I'm Mary. I'm Kathleen Hannafin's daughter.'

I told her about the name and address on my birth certificate, and about the adoption. I heard the doorbell ring – that'd be the first guest.

'Well,' she said, 'we've been waiting for this for years. You've certainly taken your time.'

From my chair in the back room with the door angled open, I could just see that it wasn't a guest but a delivery of food.

'I'm your cousin,' she said.

Nobody in the family knew about the baby. Except for Margaret of course, and Kathleen and Bill. And then, she said, she'd known too.

There was an awkward but decisive pause.

'I'm not going to tell Margaret,' she said, 'because this is a difficult time.'

'You're not going to tell Margaret?'

'I'm not going to tell her because she's going into hospital tomorrow for an operation.'

'I thought she . . . I'd no idea,' I said for the second time in an hour, although everything was suddenly the other way about.

Mary Hannafin laughed and addressed me by my first name.

'If you'd any idea how far from dead she is . . . I suppose that's what you mean, isn't it? She's a lively seventy-year-old living in west London, and Margaret and me, we're very close. She's Kathleen's sister, you see – she's my auntie Margaret.'

She said there were brothers and sisters. Margaret had five other children in all. I didn't ask when or whether she'd been married.

'And at the last count you have about twenty nephews and nieces.'

It was like a well-administered blow to the head. I had difficulty following the rest of the conversation. I asked about the operation. Mary Hannafin told me that Margaret would be out of hospital by Christmas.

'So am I,' Mary said, when I told her I was a little overwhelmed.

'So she just rang you, did she, Mrs Moore?'

'That's right,' Mary said.

'But I didn't leave her this number.'

'Yes, but I told her how to use the call trace on her phone. How did you get her number?'

I told her about the people-search site on the web. The doorbell went. She asked me how old I was.

'Fifty, and you?'

'I'm fifty-nine,' she said, 'but I'm told I don't look it.'

There were people coming through the hall and I pressed a hand to my ear to fend off the noise of greetings and laughter.

Then it was a case of crawling back through an immense feeling of chaos to the subject of Margaret's operation. It was routine, evidently, but it would be a shock to Margaret to know I'd made contact and it was best to leave off telling her until she was on the mend. Some time in the New Year. Mary might want a number for me at home.

'Yes, but I've got it, haven't I, from Edie?'

I took down her address – Mary Hannafin lived in Slough – and a number where I could reach her. Then we hung up.

The food was laid out on the plates and the plates were set on the table. The wine was ready to roll and I helped myself to a glass as I told my hosts what had just happened. They asked me to go back over the conversation with Mary, but when I couldn't remember whether she was a niece, an aunt or a cousin, I felt the whole conversation crumbling away in the telling, as though it might never have happened. A moment later I wasn't sure it had.

The guests were soon arriving at a steady rate and the nervous anticipation of the early evening gave way to a spacious, easy conviviality, which drifted up through the house. The pale lights shone on the Christmas tree between the tall windows of the main room. On the table, a charger full of pastries gave off the sweet smell of cinnamon.

I returned to the phone in the small room at the back and rang the number Mary had given me.

'You again,' she said.

I wasn't quite sure whether any of this was the way it seemed. Could we go over a few of the facts once more? The key was Mackenzie Close, wasn't it? Yes, she said, it was where she'd spent several years, in her childhood, with Bill and Kathleen, and Kathleen's sister Margaret. There was no doubt that the address on the birth certificate was the place she knew, and the place Margaret was staying when she became pregnant for the first time. No doubt, either, that the first child went up for adoption.

'I've known about you most of my life,' Mary said again. 'I was nine when all this happened and bit by bit I got to understand it.'

'Right. And if you're Kathleen's daughter and Margaret's niece, that makes you and me . . .?'

I'd always been slow to decipher the map of elementary kinship.

'I told you. We're cousins,' she said. 'You'll have to brush up on who fits where before you meet us lot, or else you'll be very confused.'

The voice was mocking, self-assured and happy. She said a little more about the half-brothers and half-sisters.

'Yes, but I'm still . . . I've no way of knowing if any of this is true.'

'Sweetheart, what can I say?' Mary Hannafin replied. 'It's all true.'

XIII

Feasts

The train left Waterloo at a leisurely pace.

I felt perfidious and blue, slinking away with my piles of documents from the Family Records Centre, notebooks full of Walshes, Hannafins, Drews, Burtons, Palfreys, and a brusque record of the mysterious, untraceable name 'Maureen Withcombe', scrawled on a bit of paper somewhere in my bag. It was as though I'd pilfered a fragment of a story that belonged to the city and nowhere else, helping myself to the public record in order to indulge a private whim.

A few minutes out of the station and the city threw me a bright, intelligible morning, not yet nine o'clock. We trundled away from the Thames and I felt a pang of regret, a quick hankering west, back and to my right, a part of me struggling upriver to meet Colin at the mooring near the village and load the Saturday shopping into the dinghy.

The London Eye was a glorious intrusion on the skyline, gone as you saw it, almost; then St Thomas's; and a few moments later the pale redbrick buildings of the Marine Society, an institution that had intrigued me as a boy – among its good works since the middle of the eighteenth century was the raising of orphans and children of the poor 'and thousands who, if they had not thus been rescued from destitution, ignorance and vice, would probably have followed the paths of idleness and infamy'. The buildings stood with quiet assurance, surrounded by newer blocks and cheap-looking warehouses, the general debris of Lambeth.

When I pulled away from the window and sat back, I was at the top of the Eye, surveying the grandeur of a city on the water, gleaming in the sunlight, somehow Margaret's city more than anybody's. A settlement on a river – though the river had become incidental, a stately, manageable heirloom, burnished by the morning light, something to show off, now that London itself rode high on a tide of its own devising. The draught of its wealth, real and contractual, could displace a small ocean. It was glamorous, beautiful, ruthless: a vast place that no longer seemed to need the sociability of the Thames.

A moment later, my vantage point on the London Eye narrowed in to a bizarre monochrome vision of the old White City Exhibition. The Flapper was going up and down somewhere above the Algerian gardens, or the Irish village, years before Margaret or Colin or Maureen or Rosemary, or anyone on my mind just now, had been born. And yet there was Margaret Walsh on her own at one end of the ride, and Maureen on her own at the other. They rose and fell in stately contention above a pale-brown vista at the western margins of the city, gazing towards Slough. Their expressions were those of model matriarchs publicising an imperial levy or an efficacious remedy for ringworm.

I hadn't asked Mary Hannafin where Margaret Walsh would have the operation. Hammersmith, perhaps, or St Mary's Paddington.

Our Christmas tree was bare. The lower branches took the placid glow of the hearth at the other end of the room, where the logs burned evenly. I felt in my pockets, found my train tickets and laid them on the fire. Outside there was a mild frost, just below zero at a guess. I was richly tired, happy to be home. As I watched the tickets blaze, I felt a curious presence at my back, a brisk animal movement beneath the tree, streamlined and cautious, like that of a large dog, or a wolf, slinking quietly under the lower branches. After it settled, I seemed to see the head of a boy, Margaret's first boy, sunk in its ice-clotted flank. He would sleep beneath the tree for a night and a day with his head in the creature's fur. And I'd watch over the two of them, like a conscientious father.

Our children appeared in their pyjamas and we started to place the decorations.

There were a few people to talk to on the phone. The Palfreys could call off the Twilight Barking. And I spoke to Peter Privett. I didn't make contact with John. Peter would tell him anyway. An email to Jess Hewitt.

Early in the New Year, Mary was in touch. Margaret's operation had been a success. She hadn't liked to say when we'd first spoken, but the doctors had found a cancer on the lung. In any case, the news was good. The frail, invisible young friend from years back appeared as Mary spoke. She was still in difficulty, only the difficulty was less obscure than it had been to the boy playing by the river, and the girl in question was now much older even than Nancy.

I checked Mary's address in Slough. I wrote to her soon after – a long curriculum vitae, dull, but clear enough to give an honest, cheerful picture.

Three weeks later, Mary rang again. Margaret knew about what had happened. Mary had shown her the letter. She was sort of upset but pleased, said Mary, really very pleased.

It was the best sort of February day in London, an import from childhood, with skies rushed in from Colorado, the blue of summer through a muslin chill, a few elegant contrails to the west. There was the snow besides, a fresh fall the evening before, and I climbed up out of the tube station to find two long belts of white, almost undisturbed, under a sparkling patina of frost that ought to have melted. The meeting was set for noon. I was early, and paced around the green cabmen's shelter on Warwick Avenue, then up and down the row of taxis parked in the reservation. There was almost no traffic. A bit past noon I began to get edgy. I had a number for Mary's mobile and took a look about for a phone box. A couple more minutes and it was obvious that Margaret had decided to back out. I could see how it went. No, she'd said firmly, and not appearing very co-operative. Mary said, What do you mean, no? You have to now. She said, I don't have to do anything if you please, Mary, I'm just out of hospital. Mary said, It's ten past twelve and if you're not coming I'll go on my own. She said, You go on your own then, would you, Mary.

Mary said, 'Hello, stranger.'

It was a cautious, dependable formula.

They'd been stepping slowly, arm in arm, on the trudged-down causeways of icy pavement, to come around the church of St Saviours. I'd spotted them soon enough, even without my glasses, and moved quickly towards them, thinking three on this opaque, risky terrain is better than two – quick or she'll slip and that'll be the end of everything. I bent across to kiss Mary on the cheek, and Margaret, who seemed small and frail, and now I was intent on our feet, all six, as we slithered up Clifton Gardens arm in arm, with Margaret in the middle. If I was a steadying hand to one side of her, how was it I had the impression of being steadied myself?

There was a restaurant at the end of the road. We sat at a small circular table. Margaret and Mary ordered a bottle of white wine. They smoked. No, not any more, I said.

'That's good,' said Margaret. She intended to stop any day now. 'But we're a little nervous, you can imagine.'

It was an Irish accent; the voice was deep.

I could imagine, I said.

'I expect you are too.'

Yes, a little nervous.

'I bet you are.'

Her hair was blonde going on white, cut short, just down over the ears, and she wore a fringe about the middle of the forehead. Age had reduced her mouth a little – she was seventy-one, she said – and it was the only elusive feature of the younger woman I could otherwise see clearly. The rest was delicately drawn: she had a fine, angular nose; bright blue eyes, alert but undistracted. The face was robust, despite that delicacy, and of course she'd lost weight since her operation.

I could read no mark of character in this stranger's aspect – no visible strengths or weaknesses, no inclination to caprice or stubbornness, no obvious hint of kindness or unkindness. I could see no likeness to any of my children, or to me, and I was uncertain whether I felt relief or disappointment. 'Feeling', it was clear, would have to bide its time: a crowd of emotions were queuing for the doors to open, though I couldn't say when that would be, or whether there might be a sudden cancellation. The main thing now, for all of us, was to make it to the other side of lunch.

Mary excelled at small talk. She wove a careful, politic commentary through our exchanges about Margaret's health, such-and-such a doctor, such-and-such a treatment, feeling better, the decline of the health service, how was the health care where I was? I could see myself in my cousin straight away, the physical likeness, I mean. She was tall, she had a long face with plenty of nose and forehead. There was a recognisable cast to her eyes, part faraway, part sceptical, that I didn't care for in photos of myself, but which suited her well. Later on, when she stood up, I caught sight of her in a mirror near the bar and had, for an instant, to work out how on earth the reflection showed me moving across the room even though I was seated. But by then we'd been drinking and if some things had become a little confused, the rest was getting clearer and easier.

Margaret had a rough sense, from what I'd written to Mary, how I'd gone about looking for her. I couldn't remember if I'd let on in the letter that I'd assumed she was dead, but I said so now, made a joke of it: on the contrary, and so on.

'Please God,' said Margaret, without a hint of piousness in that voice you'd never mistake for someone else's. A compelling voice, I found, which kept the tempo of conversation from falling away.

There were the numerous Margaret Walshes to talk about. She enjoyed that. There was the taciturnity of the Hannafins. She liked that, too. There was Mackenzie Close and the puzzle of the Chain Stores.

'I was working at Woolworth's,' she said. 'On the counter. The Edgware Road, wasn't it, Mary?'

Mary thought it was.

There were the Palfreys and the Wests and the other neighbours, but she didn't recall them. Neither did Mary, who mentioned a few names I hadn't come across in the rolls.

Margaret's sister Kathleen and Kathleen's husband Bill had got the flat in the 1940s. Margaret had come over from Ireland to join them and find work. The three of them had lived there with Mary and her two brothers. Bill Hannafin worked for the railways. Kathleen stayed at home. Many of their friends were from Ireland and a good deal of those were family. In London they'd stuck together. I asked about Edward Stephen Walsh. He was Margaret's brother, an older brother – he'd been eligible to vote – and yes, he'd been at the close briefly. He was dead now.

The Palfreys had said something about taking in children. Mary couldn't imagine what that had been about, but after a time she thought perhaps there'd been a confusion to do with the fact that she and her brothers had been away for a while when they were quite young. The neighbours would have seen them go and, after a lengthy absence, come back again, and they'd have concluded that Kathleen took in children from time to time.

Why had they been away? Kathleen had fallen ill with tuberculosis. In those days, British Railways had a home for the children of employees in distress. Mary and her brothers were sent to a large house in Derbyshire for the best part of a year. Mary had vivid memories of the place. She'd been homesick, but happy there.

Kathleen Hannafin in Slough had niggled me, I explained, and in the end I'd picked up the phone and called Edie Moore. I asked Mary about Harriet and Conrad, who'd had the flat where John Webb first set eyes on Margaret. Good times in Kensal Rise, said Margaret. I spoke of Peter and Lilian Privett and John Webb, and how I thought there'd been a breakthrough, in the shape of someone who actually remembered Margaret. They laughed. She'd no memory of John Webb. She'd never heard of Peter and Lilian Privett and she couldn't for the life of her think why the address in Chesterton Road was on my birth certificate. We circled for a time, but there was no explanation.

Harriet and Conrad?

Harriet and Conrad were dead, Mary thought.

'Chesterton Road, Ladbroke Grove . . . that was old Christie's neck of the woods,' said Margaret. 'He was before your time.'

'The murderer,' Mary said.

I didn't like to say I'd felt Christie presiding contemptuously over my efforts to find any evidence of Margaret in Ladbroke Grove.

We kept the wine moving at a good rate, with Margaret holding her own and the day persisting brightly through the plate glass at the end of the restaurant, the glitter and sunshine buffing the brick fronts above the shops on the other side of the street.

'You've been all over,' said Margaret, 'with your job and that.'

I'd travelled a fair bit in the 1980s and 1990s and I'd mentioned this in the letter I'd written to Mary.

'Here and there,' I said, 'but never to Ireland.'

'We'll have to take him, won't we, Mary?'

Margaret had done a fair number of jobs herself over the years. The last time she'd worked, a while before her operation, she'd been cleaning for an elderly lady, an easy walk from her own place. Where was that? I asked. Margaret lived in a council flat about ten minutes from the restaurant.

Now that the food was gone, and most of the other customers had disappeared, more wine was ordered and the photos came out. The siblings first: two brothers, the older in his mid-forties, a stocky, strong-looking man with a preoccupied expression, a passionate Chelsea supporter, his mother said; another in his mid-thirties, more affable and easygoing, big again, with large, gentle eyes. There was a third boy, whom she didn't talk about much, in his early thirties.

'But if you ever want a ticket to a Premiership game or a West End sell-out,' Margaret said, 'he's your man.'

My half-brothers had fourteen children between them.

I hadn't anticipated brothers: they were never in Maureen's nonsensical script. But sisters had been a long-standing, intimate absence from my life. The photos showed a pair of twins in their early forties, tall women with long blonde hair. The resemblance to Margaret was obvious in both – one a mother at home, the other a playgroup worker. I went over Maureen's story of the girls she might have adopted, but it seemed ridiculous to Margaret, and I imagine it made her angry.

The sisters, she went on to say, had six children. Altogether I was set up with a deal of nephews and nieces.

'Now are you sure you're so pleased you've found me?' she said. 'And all my baggage?'

I thought how pale she looked and what a strain this must be for her.

'If we add in your three,' said Mary, 'your mother's now the proud owner of twenty-three grandchildren.'

We touched our glasses and drank from them, my cousin by blood, her aunt and me.

'And you're impressed,' said Mary, 'because I know I am.'

Then we were looking at one another for a moment or two, quite unprepared for what we might discover, unsure what the next step ought to be. Margaret set one foot down, gingerly, on the track that could turn to quicksand at any point.

It was a weight off her mind, she said finally. I'd had a good life, hadn't I?

This was true.

'It wasn't so terrible, then,' she said.

'Not at all terrible,' I said.

I'd made it a rule that I wouldn't ask her anything directly about the adoption. But she wanted to speak about giving the baby up.

It was Kathleen and Bill who'd decided that adoption was the only course. She concurred during the pregnancy, but after eleven days with her first child in Hammersmith Hospital, the final scenes had been intolerable.

She'd weathered the punitive ways of the nurses, she explained: 'Always "Miss Walsh this" and "Miss Walsh that", making a big thing of the "Miss", till I thought, Christ, you know, to hell with the lot of you.' She'd got through the discomfort, and the induction with castor oil and orange juice, and then the labour, but she hadn't reckoned with the pain of separation.

When they came to get the child, she told Kathleen and Bill they couldn't, she wouldn't have that, she'd changed her mind. But Bill insisted, and there was an end of it.

'They said, "You'll forget about it, you'll get used to it sooner or later, and you'll start your life over again." Which is what I did. What else could I do?'

171

People speak of mothers giving up their children for adoption, but you could just as well think of it the other way about, as the baby abandoning the mother.

Maureen loomed briefly, ghostly, at my side. My carer, my real-world mother. How much easier it was to be with a mother who hadn't raised you – how congenial, what fun – than it was to have spent a lifetime as a disobliging son. If there was anything I'd found hard to bear, it was going to a restaurant with Maureen and Colin. Maureen would drink too much and Colin would offend the staff – 'this meal is a disgrace' and so on – as if a person didn't have to fill his stomach one way or another. But what if I'd met them only once, over lunch, like this? They'd have seemed bracingly eccentric. Being adopted, I wanted to say to Margaret, you were always in a state of extenuation, you slipped in and out of things. A stern judge of character would have called it disingenuousness. I'd come to think of it as a way of life.

Mary was smoking like an off-duty detective.

'And after you'd . . . after we'd gone our own ways,' I found myself saying. 'What became of you?'

'Oh, you know,' Margaret says in her deep voice, with that prepossessing, lyrical Irish thing I'd meant to resist. 'You know,' she said again, 'this and that.'

The pallor had gone from her face. She took my hand and we held on, fingers and thumbs, discreetly. She was using my first name a lot. It was like the constant, regular tug of a line, pulling me forwards, I felt, until at last I asked her where the name had come from. I'd thought of 'Jeremy' as Colin and Maureen's choice.

'No,' she said, moving into a higher, ironic register, 'it was my name.'

'You mean his name,' said Mary.

'Whatever, Mary,' she said. 'The one I gave him before . . .'

Before I lit off.

'Now, tell me,' she said, like a venerable old lady at a function for younger relatives, 'are you having a good time?'

We drank more. It was becoming easy, and the three of us lay back a little into the rhythm of the occasion. I asked if she'd married.

She had, in 1960, a few years later than I'd pursued her through the green registers.

And now I broke the rule by asking if she'd ever met my adoptive parents. No, she never had. Decidedly not. Bill and Kathleen would have made the switch, assuming there'd been no third party at the point of delivery. And on that score, she knew nothing.

Back again to Lilian Privett. Did she recall the name or the person?

She thought not. It was miserable and bleak, the way it had gone: a chaos from which she'd had to scrabble out intact, and then put the episode behind her.

I hadn't raised the matter of paternity, but now we had one another firmly by the hand, she made a hasty approach, wanting – I thought – to get the subject out of the way. We stumbled over it together, with me asking yes, but was he a waiter on a ship?

'Not at all,' she said. 'He wasn't a man to go to sea, so far as I know.'

'What use are they anyhow?' Mary asked.

'What's that?' I said.

'Men,' she said gaily.

It was some sort of signal that we should go no further. Mary and Margaret were much amused. And the father, whoever he was, was laughed out of court: a hazy, indifferent figure turning and vanishing deeper into the obscurity from which they'd never meant him to step.

Margaret returned to her marriage and her other children. She spoke of her fondness for Ireland and her ease in London. Altogether she gave the impression of being an easy person, even in a testing situation of the kind we were in, and when Mary brought out the next round of photos, showing Margaret and Kathleen on the QE2, with Margaret looking healthier than she was now, and fuller in the face, I could see the ease there, too.

'Your brothers and sisters don't know about you,' Mary said, and Margaret gave me a plausible smile.

The senior boy was the head of the clan, and some courage would be required of Margaret to let him know there was an older sibling. He'd had a tough few years and now they were behind him, but he had his head down, with six children to manage. The other brothers, one at any rate, and the sisters, one at any rate, might receive the news of a half-brother with more equanimity. It would all happen in time. Or it wouldn't.

There was no need, I ventured, to do anything on my account.

Mary was visibly relieved.

'No, Mary,' Margaret protested with a slow shake of her head. 'It'll have to be done.'

Her voice was, if anything, lower. She looked down at her drink and then up at me. Part of her must have wished I hadn't appeared out of nowhere in this way. The other part had me tight by the fingers.

'All in good time,' said my new cousin Mary, the family diplomat.

We drank, and kept up the talk about Margaret's children, as though to muster them about her now. She'd been happy to find out that her firstborn had come good. But hard on that feeling, new kinds of difficulty were taking shape.

Who to tell and when: this was one of several delicate areas we'd crossed, with very few casualties, in the space of a couple of hours, although the fact that I'd become a secret again wasn't lost on me.

'Tell me,' said Margaret, still concerned that the party should go well, 'are you really having a good time?'

I put my arm round her shoulder. Early afternoon was sliding away towards late afternoon and the waiters were showing the first signs of restlessness.

What was said of the children in general suggested they didn't hold with the idea of roots – unlike Mary, who felt Irish through and through – and this much we had in common. When Mary asked me did I know how Irish I was, Margaret took me by the hand again.

'Of course he doesn't, Mary.'

'No,' said Mary, 'but I just thought . . .'

There was the great scrum-half Mick Doyle. I'd seen him at

Twickenham – an exciting, insatiable player – when I was a boy. He'd later played for Ireland, and I'd carried a torch for the team. Was that enough to be going on with? Then, too, there were the writers you think of as Irish, however they'd thought of themselves. And Colin used to sing when I was a boy: there were two or three Irish songs slipped in among the music hall numbers I'd learned.

Mary laughed and asked for a refill. She was exuberant and funny. None of us could quite believe what had happened.

When I began to resist the pull of the alcohol and tried to figure Margaret and Mary's descriptions of the family, it was clear how vastly separated we'd become by circumstance.

Turning what Margaret and Mary said about my three brothers into a generic profile, I could make out the shape my life would have taken if I'd stuck around. I'd have been the father of five children (4.3 to be exact) conceived with two partners. I'd have left school at an early age. I'd be living, on average, no more than a half-hour walk or a short bus ride from my mother's. The odds were against my setting foot outside England very often: London would have been an unconditional and rewarding fact of life. I'd have made jokes about our mother's Irishness – nothing cruel, a tug of the leg now and then – and regarded myself as a pure English product, by disposition and default. A lot of what went for the brothers was true of the sisters, from what I could tell – including the fact that they, too, lived close to their mother.

Yet any more detailed account of the differences between the person I was and the one I might have been by remaining in the clan was pointless. The serious distinction between Margaret's people and me, the thing that set us apart, I suppose, was the fact that I'd been able to pile up wealth, incapable of functioning in the world without the thought that it was there to fall back on. The gratifications of surplus were not so insistent, or possible, for my brothers and sisters. Nor were they for Margaret. There'd been accumulation, but not the kind you could liquidate if you needed to. Whatever else she was, whoever else she'd been as a working person, Margaret preferred to think of herself as a daughter, a sister, a mother and finally a grandmother. To that extent, she was laying claim to a way of life. Family was the abundance she'd stored up, whether she'd meant to or not. You could say it was what she owned, or you could say it was all she had.

But I didn't have to say anything. I'd felt edged into a wonderful, puzzled reticence, robbed of the words for things I knew well: difference or affinity by social group and background; wealth and poverty, having and making do, and the gradations in between. Margaret and I had stumbled through the battle lines of the British class system like a pair of ragged picnickers – and now we were spreading the rug over the grass, determined to ignore the great forces all around us manoeuvring for position.

Perhaps some new pressure – the pressure of 'blood' or 'nature' – was responsible for the momentary lapse in my habits of describing people. But that seemed unlikely. What would blood prove if our meeting had turned out badly, as reunions can? Supposing Margaret had thought me a callow little prig who knew nothing about real life? If the blood-tie could bring love and loyalty to bear, it could also be an engine of bitter disappointment.

And for a moment, in a flash of intelligence I never quite regained, the process Margaret and I had begun turned into a second adoption. A two-way adoption without rules, of course, since either of us could pull out without prior warning, and at any point. But otherwise the similarity was striking. And if blood could go either way, then it wasn't the main consideration, any more than it was in old-fashioned infant adoption, where natural and social identities were reinvented in a single fluent movement.

What mattered was to want to engage with another person, and to continue believing this was a good thing to do. Margaret and I were embarked on an experiment that had begun as a matter of chance, whose outcome would be determined largely by chance. For as long as we proceeded with care, it was likely to go well.

'Excuse me,' she said, 'but if you're having a good time, and you say that you are, then you won't object if I do what I shouldn't and smoke another cigarette.'

She reached across for Mary's packet.

'Tell me,' Mary asked, 'is this at all how you imagined it?'

I hadn't imagined it.

'But weren't you nervous?'

'It's fine,' said Margaret with an air of confidence, as though she were dragging us away from slippery ground. 'We were all nervous. You were, Mary. And I was, I'm sure. And he was, I suppose. And now we're none of us nervous.' She pointed her finger at me and laughed. 'You're a nosy prat, by the way,' she said. 'That's my honest opinion.'

'She means,' Mary said, 'that someone like you who gets to find someone like her after all these years is a proper little busybody.'

'That's exactly what I mean,' Margaret said.

We were pleasantly high on the drink. I looked at Margaret's face, then at Mary's, and tried to fix my own in the mirror. We lingered over the glittering remains of our feast – the red paper napkins hunched beside the bright empties and the half-done glasses – while the waiters circled. I was sitting at the westerly edge of my life, where no story could ever again surprise me by the manner of its ending, and I was holding the hand of my first mother, also my last.

Outside, the light was orange and the day was old. By the time we'd dealt with the bill, the other tables were reproachfully clean. I ordered a cab for Mary Hannafin and the former Miss Walsh.

XIV

The Falling Boy

From time to time I spoke to Margaret and Mary on the phone. I
went to London again and we ate in the same place. We trod carefully. It was a piece of good fortune, and perhaps a tribute to us,
that we got along. There were more photos, more tentative
exchanges of information, but nothing too difficult. We were all
three of us given to frankness, but when we met or spoke, we preferred to move slowly around things, like dancers in rehearsal, on
a stage where the set is still no more than a series of chalk marks
on the floor. For my part, I was happy.

In due course, I opened my computer file on Margaret. I read
over the paragraph I'd struggled with in London, wiped it entirely, and began again from scratch, piecing together what I knew
about my natural mother: there was much more now than there'd
been when I left London at the end of the previous year:

> Margaret Walsh was born in Limerick in 1932. She was the
> weaker of twin girls, though it was her sister who died not
> long after birth. Her mother, Christina Downey, was in
> domestic service as a seamstress when she married Margaret's
> father, Patrick, a stern man and a daunting head of the family
> – Margaret and the other children called him 'sir' – who earned
> his living as a tailor. Not much of a living, as it happened. The
> family were tenants in a row of cottages on the edge of town
> and depended for much of their income on the pigs they kept.
> When time came to settle the annual account with the local
> store, one of the pigs would be sold to slaughter.
>
> Margaret grew up as the eighth of thirteen children. The old-
> est, John, was a fighter who used to work the boxing booths at
> the local fairs. The Hannafins, a family with a big crop of boys,
> lived sixty miles away in Tralee. The Walshes and Hannafins

178

were on good terms and in due course Margaret's sister Kathleen – the third of the Walsh children – married one of the boys, who was on military service in Limerick. There was no economic future to speak of in that part of the south and it was obvious to the children of both families – to Kathleen and William especially – that before long they'd have to move away.

With the outbreak of war, Irish migration took an unforeseen turn. Briefly, in 1939 and 1940, the number of Irish leaving Britain for home was larger than the number entering Britain for work. But the demand for manpower was irresistible. Within a couple of years there were three thousand people leaving Ireland every month and arriving in Britain. Two or three of the Walsh and Hannafin boys enlisted, some, like William Hannafin, in the Irish army, others in the RAF and the British army. There was a pang of conscience about enlisting in the British services: in a well-known travesty of British military justice that caused anger and dismay in the family, Patrick Downey, Christina's brother, had been executed outside Salonika in 1915 for insubordination. He'd refused to fall in for a fatigue, and then to put on his cap. Even so, joining the forces was an obvious way out of poverty. The factories, too: arms and aircraft especially. By 1945 William, Kathleen, several Walshes and at least one other Hannafin boy were in Britain, or serving overseas.

Margaret saw out the war from Limerick, with a diminished band of brothers and sisters. Her father was already dead. She left for England in 1947 and found work as a chambermaid. It isn't clear where she lived between her arrival and the year that William and Kathleen appear on the electoral roll as residents at 43 Mackenzie Close.

She returned at least once to Limerick while her mother was still alive and remembered buying a pair of suitcases to take with her. At the time, suitcases were the status symbol of the successful migrant worker and would have been an essential item even if they were half-empty. Margaret's were both full. She remembered the perplexity she'd caused at home by adding toothpaste to the family shopping list during one of her return visits.

When Christina died, it was clear that the rest of the children would have to head for England. The arrangements were made and the last pigs sold. By 1950 or 1951, she was settled on the White City Estate and working in Woolworth's. It was about this time that her brother Edward, who was in the services, lived at the close. Within a year or so, he'd married and moved on; and she had borne her first child, whom William and Kathleen persuaded her to send for adoption.

The Walshes and Hannafins were part of a big Irish community based in Cricklewood, Kilburn, Shepherds Bush and Hammersmith. The 1951 census found more than a million Irish-born residents in Britain, a quarter of those living in London and the south-east. Irish labour was still in demand and even though the war had put migrants from Ireland into a wider range of jobs, a majority remained in construction work and domestic service. A couple of the Hannafin and Walsh boys went in and out of the building trade. William, meanwhile, had found work as a shunter on the railways.

Margaret left her sister's and gave birth to another son, five years after the first. She was still single, but she decided not to put the second boy up for adoption. By now there were Walshes settling to the west of London. Stephen Walsh, the youngest of Margaret's brothers, who'd been stuck with an aunt in Dublin after their mother's death, had managed to get out in 1953, and settled in Staines. Christie Walsh, an older brother, was in Slough. John was in the West Country. Margaret stayed on in London and in due course married an Englishman. She gave birth to twins in the early 1960s. A pair of girls.

Not long afterwards, Margaret began working as a messenger in Whitehall, delivering office mail in the ministries. William and Kathleen went out to Slough, but Margaret stayed put. Slough wasn't a great distance by train. Meanwhile, most of her brothers and sisters were comfortably within range. And there were the Hannafin boys, scattered around and producing children of their own.

Margaret gave birth to a fifth child in the mid-1960s and a

sixth a few years later. Then the grandchildren began arriving, the first in the 1970s, after which there was no let-up. In 2003 she discovered there were three more, bringing the total to twenty-three. By then she was a thin and diligent matriarch with a weakness in her lungs, a good head for drink, a council flat in Maida Vale and a memory stretched to capacity by more than thirty birthdays it wouldn't do to overlook. She was sure her first child hadn't been born on the fifth day of July or the seventh, as rumour and convention had it, but on the fourth.

I printed off the entry and read it over. Nothing I had to say could take the measure of this person, or the weight of affection I'd started to feel. And this summary of her life? Hadn't it been the original objective? Something specific, a few details set down on paper about my natural mother. Now the fact that she was alive seemed to suggest that I'd cheated in some way. In any case, she was perfectly able to tell her own story. I placed the pages on top of the notes and certificates I'd accumulated in London and went to the kitchen in search of the right kind of plastic bag.

A few minutes later, I braced myself for the muddle of the loft, where I always ventured with reluctance and only found what I was looking for by chance, which is to say by not looking for it, or being intent on a different errand. Which must have been what happened. For in an exchange of rare precision and simplicity, I consigned one bag to the disorder of my upstairs life and came back down with another, rather important bag that I hadn't been thinking about. Though clearly I had.

For a day or two I let it lie. Then the vague hope of recovering the 'ivory' bible with Haydn Wood's inscription got the better of me.

Among the consolation prizes there was a hairbrush, a faded Polaroid photo of a small dog and a 1998 desk diary with no appointments. Also a photo of Maureen and Colin, thirty or forty years earlier, doing nothing in particular at a golf club, somewhere in Berkshire, I guessed. Finally, two pieces of paper that Peter must have got from his own files and put in the bag. They were of different sizes, but laid together and folded as if to fit into an envelope. The shorter one was a spare copy of Colin's death certificate – I'd done the honours at Colin's death and had probably sent this duplicate to Peter. The longer one was, as he'd promised, a copy of Maureen's birth certificate. I opened it out and flattened it carefully on my desk.

Maureen's birth was recorded by an Interim Registrar in Wandsworth, in what was then the County of London. She was born in Streatham, well south of anywhere I knew or understood in the city, on 21 July 1916. Only Maureen wasn't her given name. She was registered as Minnie Louie Withcombe, and would have been named after her mother, 'Minnie Withcombe formerly Pike'. The family lived in Letchworth Street, Tooting. Minnie's father was a Godfrey Withcombe. Under column six, 'Rank or Profession of Father', was the description: 'Wine and Spirits Merchants' Carman'.

My notion was that she'd been born in Mitcham, but now I could see that the family, or some of it, must have moved there later: the population of Mitcham had doubled in the first ten years of the century and from 1910 to the beginning of the 1930s there'd been a lot of new housing in the area. I might have phoned John Webb and asked about Maureen's parents, which I'd failed to do on the two visits I'd paid him, and whether she had brothers or sisters, but in any case, I knew enough now to send her off for the last time. And I could hear her saying, 'Shall we have a little something first? I do so fancy a noggin.'

I opened a bottle of wine and set it by the stove.

For as long as I could recall, Colin had wanted his ashes thrown in the river, but Maureen hadn't let on what she'd like done with hers. After the cremation, they'd gone to Peter and his wife, who were puzzled how to proceed. I'd been tempted to suggest putting them in a carrier bag and handing them to me: I'd have disposed of them without much fuss. Now I was less facetious, having learned about her 'incredible journey' – a respectable tour of the British social landscape, up the precipitous inclines swiftly and suddenly, as though attached to a pulley, then along a ways, and finally down a little, all of which seemed admirable and strange.

In her position, I'd have tried to move about a bit, too. But there'd been no need. The big move had been arranged on my behalf.

And it was all so unlike my Margaret. Which wasn't to say that Margaret had remained where she was. From Limerick to London was a major upheaval, but perhaps without the cultural shock that Maureen would have undergone. For if the Walshes were all assembled in Limerick in the 1930s, they could be found assembled again – with one or two exceptions – in west London and Slough by the early 1950s. Maureen, on the other hand, had left everyone behind, including her family and her closest friends, in pursuit of whoever it was she'd meant to become. Margaret's course, I guessed, had been far steadier. There'd been no dramatic change of tribe, no brushing over the tracks of an earlier life, nothing that would make it easy to sketch her story in a few words and give it the air of a simple, dramatic truth.

How favourable is fortune, really, to the brave or the foolhardy?

You see, you're so lucky, Maureen used to say when I was a difficult teenager. Heaven knows what would have happened to you if you hadn't come to us.

I hadn't much liked that, but I understood now that she was probably talking not only about me but about herself, as she had when she used to take me through the story of my adoption.

I drank and refilled the glass.

I'm sorry, darling, she seems to be saying, but would you top me up?

Of course, I reply. Shall we go on with the story of your remains?

Well, isn't there something a little gayer we could talk about?

You see, I persisted, in the end Peter and his wife asked us over for lunch in Cobham and then, when the children were distracted by their ice-creams, Peter's wife suggested we should tip your ashes into the lake at the end of the garden, just beyond their little swimming pool.

And as I ran my eye along the birth certificate on the table again, I imagined Maureen saying, You know it's frightful, darling, but I don't recall any of this.

Peter hadn't wanted to go down to the lake with us for the ceremony, but I went with his wife and I tipped your gritty, reconstituted cinders out of the tub. For a long time there was a lugubrious milky cloud just below the surface, like the technical bit in the old antacid commercials on ITV. And then I remembered how you hated water.

You, of course, remembered so little in the years leading up to your death. Peter said that Alzheimer's had been mentioned. In any case, you'd drunk too much, year on year, to keep a grip on your thoughts. You'd led a various life and couldn't be expected to recall the whole of it. Bits of it, certainly, you'd have had to forget, just to keep the posh manner from caving in. In the old days, you gave some wonderful performances in that vein. I'd always discouraged you from coming to see me when I was a student, but if I'd known what a star you could be, I'd have asked you more often.

It wasn't until you insisted on collecting me at the end of my final year at university – have I told you this? I've told it so often – that I realised what I'd squandered. We set off for London with a friend from college. I put him in the front with you. After a few minutes, you asked him had he enjoyed his spell at the Varsity? He was as surprised as I was.

'Yes,' you went on, 'it's what I call the best time of one's life, up at the Varsity. I expect it's disappointing to be going down.'

'Up', 'down': this was already more than enough. But a little way along the road you went one better, inclining your head towards the back of the car and asking: 'By the way, darling, what did you *read*?'

It was one of the most startling questions I've ever had to answer. There was a majestic condescension about it. Quivering in your bones, I thought at the time, was the marrow of a duchess, and yet all along you were Minnie Louie Withcombe of Letchworth Street, Tooting. True, you'd studied speech and deportment under the aegis of your first husband, and become versed in the ways of the louche and the charming by association with your second, but for a moment there you were the real thing.

184

I watch the wine swelling in the glass on the desk. I imagine it's possible to become anyone. And you did. I drink to Maureen Harding; I study your birth certificate again; I drink to Minnie Withcombe. And here's to the Interim Registrar.

You won't remember the last time we were in a car together. It was Peter's idea to bring you out from the old people's home for a barbecue. He felt, in his well-meaning way, that you ought to meet my children. The lunch had gone well. Even so, after you'd had a bit to drink, you took off on some dark assignment of your own. For an hour or more, nobody knew where you were. Peter drove around and found you a mile up the road. You had a habit of vanishing from the establishments where you were interned, or if we took you away for a light lunch in a nearby pub, of flouncing out of the ladies and blazing a trail to the middle of nowhere, often with the idea that you were making for 'home' (which of the many places you'd lived in with Graham and Colin and then on your own was that? we wondered). You'd become the fourth animal protagonist of *The Incredible Journey*, only you were doomed to travel solo.

Peter was relieved he'd found you, but you and he had so enraged one another that we decided I should take you back to your real home, the old people's home, before matters got any worse. I put you in the front passenger seat of my car and after a few miles, you asked me about Peter: 'Who was that detestable man?'

'He's your son Peter,' I said.

'I've never heard such nonsense in my life. He tried to . . .' Short pause. '. . . abduct me. Kindly take me home.'

'I'm taking you home,' I said.

Five minutes later you began hitting me over the head and shoulders with a retractable umbrella. You were terrified. You thought I was driving you to your death. There were a few years yet but in essence you were right. When you told me to let you out, I used the central locking. I urged you to calm down. You'd have ejected at sixty miles an hour and probably at ninety. You screamed and I screamed back. It was almost like being in love. It was the A3, we were in the fast lane, and once I'd thrown the umbrella into the back, you started trying to drag up the handbrake.

In Chichester, the nearest town to your incarceration, you complained of the heat and I lowered the nearside window. At a set of traffic lights, you managed, in a single rapid manoeuvre, to open the door and scurry off along the pavement. I watched aghast. You looked a bit like Mrs Thatcher – it was the tottering gait, always about to pitch you on to your face, and the shouting, which I could hear even as you made off and the lights refused to change for me.

You hurried into the forecourt of a big petrol station. I followed you around and stopped the car. I approached the attendant to ask if I could use the phone. You took a bearing at the edge of the forecourt and set off unerringly, like a dog, in the direction of the old people's home.

'Yes,' said the attendant, 'I'll get the number for you. It's Mrs Harding, isn't it? I've had her here a few times. I generally ring the home and let them ring the police.'

The last time I set eyes on you, not counting the cloudy starburst of mother resolving in Peter's lake, you were being coaxed into a police van by a pair of amiable Chichester coppers who seemed to know you well.

I drove back to Peter's to collect the family. And I kept thinking on the way that the friendly attendant at the garage reminded me of something. Coming off the A3 for Oxshott, I began to hear the traders at Covent Garden in the old days. It was 'good old Mrs H' again, the way they'd always said it, and the way the garage man had said it now, like something from a musical, a refrain that never dies. Whoever you were, you went down big in the right quarters.

The ending of *My Fair Lady* is a travesty of the way things turn out in *Pygmalion*; I'd been meaning to bring this up with you. In the musical – I've explained this to myself already – Eliza and Professor Higgins fall in love. But in the afterword to the play, Liza settles for Freddie Eynsford-Hill. The couple work hard in Liza's flower shop and in the end she has what Shaw's generation called a position.

The play is at ease with the idea of social mobility – something vigorous and proper, under the right conditions. Even so, there has to be a means of access, a communicating chamber, between Liza's first life and her second, and I've sometimes imagined it took the form of flowers. Perhaps she was in the habit of setting a vase in the dining room of the modest Eynsford-Hill apartment, where the scent got stronger as the blooms began to fade.

Did you ever say the word 'anemone' correctly? Windflower, Crowfoot family. Liza would have had it off perfectly, after her own stint in the elocution hothouse. It was the m's and n's you tended to confuse. I raise my glass to you again. Maureen Harding, the last person you became before you sank without trace, could point me towards a pretty thing and say: 'anenome.'

'You know, darling, I call it . . . an anenome.'

Yes, I'd say to vex you, but what's it for?

It's no use your sitting here all day. Where do you live?

It's gone midnight, you're seventy-something. Or you used to be. You're singing your old favourites.

To savour the last moment with you that I can make sense of, I have to recreate that sunny afternoon at Peter's before you did a runner. It was earlier in the afternoon, it was hot. You'd got caught up in the ritual of a family barbecue with only an inkling of why you were there. Could it possibly be your birthday? How old were you? Peter plied you with gin and tonic. My children seemed to you unaccountable but charming presences. You had some vague recollection of their mother. Peter put our two-year-old boy next to you at the table in the garden, under the parasol. If you listened carefully, through the bicker of moorhens on the lake, you could hear the sound of traffic coming off an A-road somewhere, buffeting the ghost of the English countryside.

I prised a slab of lamb from the griddle and put it on your plate. You set about trying to cut it.

Your hair was lank, drably plastered about your ears and neck. Your eyes were if anything smaller than I recalled, their heavenly blue was gone to the world, like the skies of the painters, which don't gaze back.

'I can't eat this, Peter,' you said, addressing no one in particular.

'Let me cut it for you,' Peter's wife suggested.

You thought: I'd like another gin and tonic.

'Yes dear, what a good idea,' you said. 'That's what I used to do for my doggies. We all found it easier cut up.'

Peter's wife took the knife and fork and sliced away at your meat. You patted the small child who was sitting next to you, as I cut up his.

'Is there any tonic water?' you asked judiciously. 'I fancy a top-up.'

'No gin then, I suppose, mother?' said Peter as he reached for the Gordon's, fixed your enormous fizzy drink and dropped in a slice of lemon.

'Thank you, darling,' you said, gazing out at the lake. 'Isn't this lovely here, Peter? We're so lucky.'

The child to your right, gingerly poised on a white garden chair, set his fingers to the edge of the table and pushed. Then he was rocking. Better not, I cautioned, from my seat to your left. And sure enough he began to plummet, slowly, like a creature in space, the garden chair tumbling with him like a damaged module. You too were in space, intently there, toying with the salad on your plate. Your gin and tonic was in front of you, and in the distance, behind it, the luminous bodies of kith and kin whose names you'd forgotten; beyond them the outer vastness of the lake.

We all watched as your hand shot over the falling chair to the falling boy. In a series of spasmodic, instinctive gestures, you'd got hold of a little wrist in one hand, then a little arm in the other, and in a trice you'd let go of the wrist so as to seize a part of the chair, as though you and he were beyond the pull of gravity. I watched him start floating back into position. We all continued looking on, frozen at our placings round a large, white plastic table where the sunlight beat down on a dish of dressed cucumber. We were like ground control technicians, thousands of miles from the pinprick drama. Moments earlier, a lifetime possibly, you'd been wondering who these children were, and what to do with the bit of barbecued meat in your mouth. Yet here you were, suddenly called on to act, levering the small boy and the vivid plastic chair back into alignment so that the mysterious mission could proceed, without a hitch, through the timeless hush all around you.

An hour later and you'd gone.

Then you were getting out of the car in Chichester. Then the local police constabulary were helping you with your enquiries. Then there was the cremation, and finally your descent into Peter's lake. Strange how you and Colin both wanted a cindery end. Strange too how it had to be followed six or seven months later by a bracing encounter with water – as though our family were some hopeless fire-fighters in a silent comedy, eager to put you out long after the moment had passed.

I returned the birth certificate to the plastic bag, along with the hairbrush and the other memorabilia.

I was trying to sleep. The hands of an elderly woman flew through thin air to grab hold of a toppling child as though her life and his depended on it. Good care. Next came the clatter of a victualler's cart drawn by a horse, or possibly a pair of horses, with Godfrey Withcombe, 'Wine and Spirit Merchants' Carman', holding the reins. Then it was Maureen, seated in her grandmother's make-believe carriage with the make-believe Dalmatians bringing up the rear. The genealogy of that fantastic image fell quietly into place. It even crossed my mind that Minnie's father would have let her up on the dray when she was a little girl. Once or twice, surely, by way of a treat.

Acknowledgements

Various drafts of this book were read by friends and relatives before it reached the publisher. They improved it greatly in the process. My thanks, above all, to Jean McNicol, Ewan Smith, John Wakefield and Mary-Kay Wilmers for close reading and advice on the manuscript. Also to Julian Birkett, Gill Coleridge, Charlotte Eilenberg, Mary Hannafin, Beth Holgate, Kevin Loader, Peter, Jenny and Briony Mathieson, Lorna Scott Fox and Stephen Walsh for numerous corrections and suggestions. At Faber, Jon Riley, for commissioning *Mother Country*, and Lee Brackstone for seeing it through. For superb archive intelligence and statutory counselling, Sue Nott. For valuable thoughts about the vicissitudes of the 'search', Stephen Cooper and Andy Ward.

The foundations of this book were laid in a talk for BBC Radio 3, one of a series called *Another Country*. The architects were Tim Dee and his colleagues in Bristol. The *London Review of Books* published a generous sample of work-in-progress.